THOMISTIC PAPERS

Thomistic Papers
1

Edited by
Victor B. Brezik, C.S.B.

CENTER FOR THOMISTIC STUDIES
University of St. Thomas
Houston, Texas 77006

Contents

v

Foreword

The Center for Thomistic Studies is a center of philosophical research and teaching, offering the master's degree and the doctorate. It differs from most other graduate schools of philosophy in that, though students may elect any area of philosophy for concentration, they are required to be familiar with the philosophy of St. Thomas Aquinas on the graduate level. The Center is convinced that Aquinas' philosophy has much to offer the world.

The Center considers publication an important part of its work. In addition to having its faculty write books and articles published elsewhere, the Center wishes to produce its own publications. Rather than produce an annual review, it has opted to make available at frequent intervals *Thomistic Papers*. This first number contains the text of six talks given at the Center by members of its faculty and Advisory Board. It is hoped that our readers will find them fruitful.

Leonard A. Kennedy, C.S.B.
Director
Center for Thomistic Studies
University of St. Thomas

Introduction

Can a collection of essays on diverse topics by different authors have any more unity than that of a conglomeration? Sound Thomism teaches that the unity of a thing follows its being. It is obviously one thing to bring six essays into existence. That was the task of the six individual authors of these essays. It is quite a different affair to reduce their independent work into some sort of unity. This is the poor editor's task.

I would be less concerned about the unity of this volume were it not also sound Thomism that nothing is understandable except in terms of its unity, as nothing is knowable if it does not partake of being. A symposium or a seminar or a colloquium is usually organized around a theme or a problem which lends some unity to the whole discussion. But what kind of unity can there be in a collection of papers delivered at irregular intervals on various subject matters such as comprise the contents of this volume? Surely no more unity than is normally found in a professional journal or periodical. I would be satisfied if no one expected more than that minimum of unity.

Yet there evidently is a suggestion of definite unity in the very title *Thomistic Papers*. These papers are all philosophical papers and while philosophy may treat of anything under the sun or above, it will treat of it from the unified perspective of philosophy. Any philosophical journal possesses at least this much unity. I propose that this volume has, in addition to such unity as a philosophical treatment gives, the further unity imparted by a Thomistic viewpoint.

These papers were all delivered at the Center for Thomistic Studies, established for the purpose of advancing and promoting philosophy as grounded in principles enunciated and discoverable in the writings of Thomas Aquinas. They all derive a basic unity from their relationship to the thought and doctrine of the Angelic Doctor. Initially, this may appear to narrow and limit the possibilities of philosophical speculation by imposing on philosophy a preconceived conformism to one thinker's outlook. But anyone acquainted with the motivation and the spirit of philosophizing of Thomas Aquinas will be somewhat reserved in reaching such a judgment. Among thinkers of all time, St. Thomas, as to motivation, stands out for his deep love for and dedication to truth; and as to his spirit of philosophizing, he speculated with an open mind to truth regardless of who gave expression to it. While on the whole he favored, from the roster of his philosophical predecessors, the basic orientation of Aristotelianism, the sole reason for his intellectual leanings is the philosophical truth he recognized in the books of Aristotle.

It is this relentless pursuit of truth from any source defining the philosophical drive and expenditure of intellectual energy of Aquinas, combined with the studied conviction that his philosophical thought provides history with an incomparable formulation of the root principles of philosophical truth, that serves as an inspiration for the endeavors of the Center for Thomistic Studies. Far from restricting philosophy to a single viewpoint, the primary motivation of the Center, following the example of Aquinas, is to seek the truth of philosophy itself and to accept the authentic expression of it from any source whatever. It is in this spirit that the teaching of Aquinas itself must be confronted. Thomism, too, merits philosophical acceptance only in terms of the compelling evidence of its truth. Truth alone is the sole business of the philosopher. Nothing else strictly defines the content of the wisdom that goes under the name of philosophy. St. Thomas, to be sure, would have it no other way.

If the Center for Thomistic Studies approaches the study of philosophy under the guidance of Thomas Aquinas as its master, it is first of all because progress in study is best made with the help of a teacher, and in the second place, because a pupil is apt to have greater trust in the direction provided by a teacher whose doctrine is reliable and whose sole personal motivation is to expound the truth. A teaching so shaped and measured by the sharp edge of truth not only has a more lasting value than less carefully hewn philosophies but also seems to offer greater possibilities for developing a more thorough and integral ordering of that accumulation of persistent truths handed on in perennial fashion by the history of philosophy.

This aim of the Center for Thomistic Studies clarifies the unifying reference to the teaching of St. Thomas characterizing all the papers filling this first volume of a proposed series. The purpose of the series is to share with the philosophic public some of the thinking and intellectual activity that it is the business of the Center to sponsor and promote. It must be borne in mind that these papers were prepared as lectures to be delivered to a mixed audience of philosophy teachers, students and non-philosophers. Only subsequently to their oral presentation were the lecturers invited to improve them for publication. In all cases but one, the lecturers were available for this and compliant as well. The single exception was Professor Anton Pegis whose death in May, 1978, was a serious loss to the Center. His entry in this volume consists of a combination of two lectures excerpted from a course of studies delivered at the Center for Thomistic Studies which was condensed from a lengthier course given previously at the University of Toronto. I am most grateful to Dr. Ileana Marculescu for the use of her helpful transcription of these two lectures from the tape recordings made at the time of the lectures. From a later transcription I myself made of the tape recordings, I have been able to contribute some corrections to her transcription and further editorialize the lectures. The lectures are presented in this volume, however, with the bare minimum of changes required to render them more legible. I am confident that Professor Pegis himself would have smoothed out the wording, if not made other revisions, before allowing the lectures to be published. My thanks are offered to his son, Richard, for his consent to their publication in this volume.

These six lectures in one way or another place the doctrine of St. Thomas in relation to contemporary thought and conditions of life. Henry Veatch, in his typically conversational and dialogic style, and perhaps somewhat piquantly, points out the apparent void left by the near-bankruptcy of contemporary philosophy, especially in the area of ethics. Thinkers like Alasdair McIntyre (*After Virtue*) and Richard Rorty (*Philosophy and the Mirror of Nature*) have been writing about this philosophical wasteland. As to ethics, Veatch proposes that a reconsideration of the natural law ethics of Aristotle and Thomas Aquinas, founded upon an understanding of "nature" otherwise than as conceived by modern science, could possibly fill the vacuity with salutary results. Acknowledging that the mathematized notion of "nature" as inherited from the Cartesian school is amoral and unsuitable as the basis of ethics, Veatch argues that in terms of "the new view of science" which does not claim to give an account of the very reality of things, there is no scientific obstacle to the philosophical acceptance of a teleological account of nature as a floor for ethical theory.

How helpful could such a nature-based ethics be in solving juridical and social questions of the present-day? In his contribution to this volume, Vernon Bourke considers the insanity plea as a case in point. Both experts and ordinary citizens have been straining to define the exact determinants of an "unsound" mind. No question but that psychologists, psychiatrists, philosophers and others engaged in the field of mental health need to agree on standards and terminology. Bourke's paper seeks in an analysis of St. Thomas' teaching on voluntariness to discover certain factors that should be taken

into account in reaching a decision about the responsible actions of a defendant charged with crime. These factors, he
thinks, deserve attention today. While seeing some illogicality
in the phrase "guilty but insane," Bourke nonetheless urges
that the insanity plea itself, for both legal and ethical reasons,
be retained in the courts.

Father Weisheipl's paper returns us to an examination of
the meaning of the word "nature," which is so central in the
paper of Henry Veatch and which now receives a more ex-
plicit analysis. As Weisheipl points out, the word *nature*
(physis) is deeply rooted in Greek philosophy, although the
concept itself differs among the ancient philosophers, particularly in the teaching of Plato and Aristotle. This difference reappears more or less in the diverse interpretation of the
Aristotelian notion made in the middle ages by Avicenna and
St. Thomas Aquinas, the former, unlike Aquinas, conceiving
nature in terms of a *motor coniunctus*, a conjoined efficient
cause accompanying the body it moves. St. Thomas remains
more faithful to the Aristotelian concept which also attributes
to nature a dynamism lacking in the static concept endemic
to the mechanistic universe of Descartes and Newton.

There is no question but that the concept of nature in
St. Thomas is cut from the metaphysical fabric of the world
as he conceives it. In his philosophy, every being is endowed
with a nature and not the least is this true of man. Granting,
however, that in the vocabulary of Aquinas, nature designates
not an inert but a dynamic principle, is there truly room in the
Thomist philosophy for an evolutionistic explanation of man
and could evolution possibly provide a total explanation of
human origin? It is precisely to the latter part of this question
that the paper on "The Descent of Man According to Thomas
Aquinas" addresses itself. What is there in the Thomist concept of human nature that remains unalterably opposed to the
prevailing materialist view of man which by many today is
taken to be the inevitable conclusion to be drawn from the
Darwinian principle of evolution? That is the question of this
paper.

The paper of Anton Pegis confronts another contemporary issue, namely, the proper understanding of "intentionality" as applied to human knowledge. Although both Husserl and St. Thomas utilize the same term, the meaning they assign to it is as far apart as idealism is from realism. In Husserl's doctrine, intentionality is inserted within the Cartesian *cogito* and becomes subjective. In St. Thomas, it is a principle of transsubjectivity and of objectification and serves to identify the knower with the world. While Pegis' paper, if he had lived longer, would no doubt have received at his hands some finishing touches, even in its present state it provides us with a superb and penetrating analysis and exhibits Pegis in some of his finest thinking.

The final paper in this volume is the lecture on "Ideology and Aquinas" by Father Joseph Owens. I have placed it at the end because in some respects it is cognate to the Pegis paper which immediately precedes it and covers some of the same epistemological ground, and also because it suitably rounds out this collection of essays by delineating the general character of Thomistic philosophy as distinct from some more recent philosophies classified as ideologies. Ideology, as Father Owens makes clear, has its historical roots in the climate of thinking stemming from Descartes where human thought is the absolute beginning of philosophy, not the sensible world, as with St. Thomas. For ideology, thought comes first but its whole meaning lies in action. In direct contrast, action, for Aquinas, is entirely meant for intellectual contemplation. Even practical knowledge, whether moral or productive, as propounded by St. Thomas, although bearing more resemblance, does not fit into the concept of an ideology. Still, as a philosophy, the doctrine of St. Thomas, in the view of Father Owens, can find some common ground for conducting dialogue with the diverse way of thinking proper to an ideology. This common ground, he suggests, is the intelligible content of the Thomistic "concept" and of the ideological "idea." Can such discussions prove profitable? Indeed, Father Owens thinks, but with limitations.

These six papers present several facets of the philosophy of Thomas Aquinas. The first two touch upon his ethical doctrine; the middle two relate to his philosophy of nature and anthropology; the last two deal with epistemological considerations. Discernible throughout is the unity of outlook which accords priority to being over thought in human knowledge, while conceiving thought itself as a way of being that enjoys an eminence among all the many ways of being. Is this a philosophical realism, or a philosophy of being? Is it Thomism? Labels can be misconstrued. St. Thomas himself did not call himself a Thomist. But he evidently did have some philosophical insights that brought the human mind face to face with reality and that have helped to open the eyes of posterity for those earnest to see *what is*. Using the insights of St. Thomas, each of these papers in its individual way comprises an intellectual effort to see better what is.

Victor B. Brezik, C.S.B.
Center for Thomistic Studies
University of St. Thomas

"Philosophy, Thou Art in a Parlous State!"

Henry B. Veatch

I

The Well-Being of Contemporary Philosophy Is Only Apparent

Is my title anything more than a downright imperti-
nence? And will not many of you object that it would scarcely
appear to you that philosophy, particularly moral philosophy,
is in a bad way at all? For superficially, it might seem that
philosophy was never better! Indeed, in just the last, comparatively few years, have we not witnessed the phenomenon
of books on philosophy—yes, great heavy books and, in the
judgment of many of us, even downright dull and tedious
books in philosophy—having actually become best-sellers?
Rawls' celebrated book on *A Theory of Justice*, and more recently Richard Rorty's *Philosophy and the Mirror of Nature*, or
Alasdair MacIntyre's *After Virtue*, and, finally and most recently of all, that incredible 750-page tome of Robert Nozick's,
Philosophical Explanations—each of these, if not an actual best
seller, has certainly been something of a media event, having
been reviewed, not just in all of the better professional jour-
nals, but also having enjoyed oftentimes front-page reviews in
the Sunday book review sections of newspapers like *The New
York Times*, the *Washington Post*, yes even in the prestigious
London Times Literary Supplement. How, then, can one say
that now-a-days what has for so long been thought to be the

poor, bedraggled, and narrowly academic subject of philosophy—particularly moral philosophy—has fallen on hard times?
Is it not rather that the times have never been better for philosophy? Yes, it's almost as if philosophy had hit the big time!

Or what of the alternative line of evidence that may be
adduced from the sudden burgeoning in recent years of interest in what might be called applied ethics? Thus almost
from the turn of the century on, in the English-speaking
world, the great names in moral philosophy were, nearly all of
them, names of thinkers who concerned themselves only with
so-called ethical theory. These were names of people like G.
E. Moore, W. D. Ross, A. J. Ayer, Charles Stevenson, et al.;
and this concern seemed to be almost exclusively with the
theoretical side of moral philosophy—with its nature and justification, and not with its practical applications in the concrete situations and conflicts of daily life. In consequence, philosophers such as these never seemed to say much that was of
interest to the general public, or even to intellectuals who
were non-philosophers. And now suddenly all of that has
changed! It's not the theory of ethics that interests people, but
its applications in all sorts of different areas of human research
and endeavor—e.g. the ethical implications of medical and
biological research, of advances in nuclear technology, of
judicial decisions, of administrative policies, of legislative
enactments, etc. Nor is it just from the side of the moral philosophers that there has been this increasing concern with the
import of ethics for such diverse fields as law, medicine,
business, public administration, etc. Nor is it so much the philosophers who have been seeking out the law schools, the
medical schools, and business schools, as rather the professional schools that have been the frequent seekers-out of the
philosophers, with a view to seeing how these latter might introduce instruction in ethics into their (the professional
schools') own curricula. Who says, then, that the moral philosophers are no better than the unwanted, almost the out-
casts, on the academic scene? Quite the contrary, they have

suddenly become something of the darlings of the academic world, sought after even by the professional schools, the law schools, the medical schools, the business schools, the schools of public administration. Yes, even outside of academia it would appear that the advice of experts in ethics and in moral philosophy is repeatedly coming now to be sought after by Congressional committees, presidential boards, all sorts of agencies of public affairs, etc.

How, then, can I possibly presume to come before you singing jeremiads about the sad state of philosophy today? For is the truth not rather that philosophers have never had it so good? But no, for appearances can be deceptive! And indeed, the present apparent good estate of modern "ethicists" and moral philosophers is just beginning to show itself to be far more appearance than it is reality. True, not too many of us, and certainly not too many moral philosophers, are aware of the fact as yet. And yet only very recently, an occasional, and sometimes even a rather well-placed voice, right within the philosophical establishment, has come out with the judgment that present-day moral philosophers are, nearly all of them, little more than "phoneys"—and this not withstanding the fact that the "phoneys" do not even know that they are "phoneys." Thus in a recent book entitled *After Virtue*, Alasdair MacIntyre, whose name is certainly one to conjure with in contemporary philosophical circles, has cruelly demonstrated that the whole gamut of present-day moral philosophy from the Utilitarians to the deontologists is by and large completely bankrupt! Oh, it's not that these philosophers don't "know" their own subject matter; it is rather that their subject matter turns out not really to be a proper subject matter at all. For what is it, after all, that ethics may be presumed to be about, particularly so far as it touches fields like law, business, bio-medicine, etc.? Is it not simply about what our human rights and duties are—what as men we ought to do and be, and how we ought to be treated and respected just as human beings?

Is Present-Day Philosophy Only Propaganda?

But now here we find the philosopher, MacIntyre, coming along and saying that present-day philosophers—i.e. not philosophers of former ages and times necessarily, but particularly present-day philosophers, and specifically in consequence of the present-day situation in philosophy—these philosophers find themselves to be basically incapable of saying what our human rights and duties really are, or even of whether they are. Oh, it is not that they do not talk readily enough, and at great length, about human rights and duties, and yet what they say seems to involve very little more than simply what their own particular little in-group of philosophers would like to think our human rights and duties are, and hence would like to have others think they are. In consequence, what MacIntyre suggests that moral philosophers now-a-days are really doing is little more than peddling certain notions of what they and their own partisans want us to *believe* our rights and duties to be, with the result that their activity as moral philosophers amounts to little more than just so much propaganda—trying to get others to *believe*: (1) that we human beings, say, have a right to equal respect, or, just the opposite, that not all men do have a right to equal respect, it being the part of justice to treat unequals unequally; or (2) that human beings—yes, even a foetus, has a right to life, or, again just the opposite, that the foetus has no right to life, it being no more than a parasite on the life of another; or (3) that human beings have inviolable entitlements to their own property, or that they have no such right to property, all property being but theft.

Now be it noted that in thus pressing this charge against just about the whole of contemporary moral philosophy—the charge, viz., that philosophy, instead of affording us anything like a knowledge of our rights and duties, amounts only to so much propaganda as to what this, that, or the other group would have us believe our rights and duties to be—this devastating charge against contemporary philosophy generally, and contemporary ethics in particular, is not a charge that needs afflict all philosophy necessarily from time immemorial. Certainly, it is a charge that it would seem rather hard to make good against a more traditional moral philosophy, like that, say, of Aristotle or of St. Thomas Aquinas. Instead, the charge is one that would seem to have a rather particular and specific validity just against present-day philosophy, and philosophy in its modern condition, if I might so put it. But why? Why is it that it is present-day philosophy that would seem to be so peculiarly obnoxious to the charge of being little more than just so much propaganda?

Still, before we attempt to give an answer to why contemporary philosophy is in this unhappy condition, let us first consider still another charge that MacIntyre would press against present-day moral philosophy. For MacIntyre insists—and apparently quite rightly—that if present-day philosophy really amounts to little more than propaganda, then the consequence must surely be that its practice can amount to little more than an exercise of a kind of Nietzschean will-to-power. For what is propaganda if not an effort at willing-to-power one's own ideas and one's own views, either enforcing them upon all others, or else somehow seducing others simply to buy them or embrace them? In other words, the philosopher's concern under such circumstances will not be with truth, in any sense of discovering truth, but rather in the sense of making it or creating it, and getting everyone else to accept it, be it either by force or by hook or by crook.

Why the Unhappy Condition of Moral Philosophy?

Very well, if, following MacIntyre, we more or less go along with the view that contemporary moral philosophy turns out to be little more than just so much "sound and fury, signifying nothing," the question now becomes one of "Why?". Why and what is there about the contemporary setting and situation in philosophy that has brought ethics and moral philosophy to its present sorry state; and which, by correcting, it might be possible for philosophy to be made whole again? Thus just by way of putting contemporary moral philosophy to a kind of test, suppose we were to put the question to either an Aristotle or an Aquinas as to just why philosophy: What, after all, might one be expected to learn from philosophy, and what is the point of it? Somehow, if one had put such a question to St. Thomas Aquinas, my guess would be that, for all of the anachronism involved in the very way the question is posed, he would have answered in a way that would have been not unlike the way Aristotle would have answered such a question, or even pretty much the way Plato or Socrates might have answered it as well: "One reason for studying philosophy"—we can imagine St. Thomas saying— "is certainly in order that a person may thereby come to learn how to live, how to be truly human. For what is philosophy if not the study of being, or of what we might call the nature of things, or the way the world is, or what the facts are? Moreover, by such a study of being or of nature or of reality, one ought to be able to gain some insight into what might be called human being, or into the nature of man, the kind of being, in other words, that a human being is. After all, if you and I are each of us human beings, then in coming to know what it is to be human, will that not mean that we should come to know what it is that is incumbent upon us to do and be as human beings—how we ought to conduct ourselves, how we ought to live as human beings, what our responsibilities are as men, what our very human nature requires of us. In other words, it is no less than the study of nature, and more specifically of human nature and human being, that should provide us with a reliable instruction as to what our moral rights and duties are. Yes, I might even offer a direct quote from St. Thomas, from his Prologue to the *Commentary on the Metaphysics:* "All the sciences are ordered toward an objective, namely man's perfection, in which his happiness consists."

And with that, why don't I remind you of those somewhat jolting words of St. Paul in the fifth chapter of the Epistle to the Ephesians: "Be most careful, then, how you conduct yourselves: like sensible men, not like simpletons. So do not be fools . . ." Just how, though, is one ever to learn what it is to be "a sensible man," as over against being a "simpleton," or a "fool"? Is not the answer to such a question simply that one comes to know such things by studying nature and reality—more specifically by studying the nature of human beings, and thus coming to learn what human excellence is, as over against human folly and failure, what the right life for a human being is, as over against one that is misdirected or corrupted or degraded?

Study Human Nature

After all, to pick a somewhat crude analogy, can't all of us, as it were, simply by studying nature, come to know the difference between a flourishing, full-grown oak tree, and one that is sickly and stunted in its growth, or between a healthy fish—say a large-mouth bass—and one that is half-starved for lack of food? And yet just how exactly did we ever come by a knowledge of that sort—i.e. a knowledge of the difference between good specimens of a certain natural kind and those not so good? Surely, we were not born with that kind of knowledge; it certainly is not anything innate. Rather it has to be from an experience of nature and, as we might say, of nature's ways that we learn to recognize a healthy or flourishing fish or tree, as over against one that is anything but flourishing.

And is it not a like case with respect to human beings, and what we might call their comparative moral perfection, or lack of it, simply as human beings? For is it not from experience of nature and of the nature of man that we learn what it is, as St. Paul says, to be a sensible man, and not a fool. Thus just recall to yourselves Plato's stirring account of Socrates' conduct at his trial, particularly of his speech in answer to his accusers. Does not one thus come to recognize in Socrates, and recognize directly from a study of the facts, so to speak, someone who was truly a wise man and an eminently human being? In contrast, consider Jane Austen's revealing sketch of the character of Sir Walter Elliott in her novel, *Persuasion*:

> Sir Walter Elliott of Kellynch Hall, in Somersetshire, was a man who, for his own amusement, never took up any book but the Baronetage; there he found occupation for an idle hour and consolation in a distressed one . . .
>
> Vanity was the beginning and end of Sir Walter Elliott's character: vanity of person and of situation. He had been remarkably handsome in his youth, and at fifty-four was still a very fine man. Few women could think more of their personal appearance than he did, nor could the valet of any new made lord be more delighted with the place he held in society. He considered the blessings of beauty as inferior only to the blessing of a baronetcy: and the Sir Walter Elliott who united these gifts, was the constant object of his warmest respect and devotion.

Now surely, no one can deny that the Sir Walter Elliott who was depicted here was nothing if not a pompous ass! True, you might say that the portrait of Sir Walter was only fictional and not real. And yet I ask you, have we not all of us come across fools like Sir Walter directly in real life—yes, no doubt the person boring you with this paper you are now reading may come across as just such a fool and an ass! But in any case, the point is that it is directly in nature and in the facts, that we come to recognize the difference between wisdom and folly in human beings, between human excellence and human shortcoming. In fact, is it not analogous to the way in which we might say that nature discloses to us the difference between excellence in fish, say, or in oak trees, as over against those not so excellent. True, the goodness of a tree or a fish is not in any sense a properly moral goodness, whereas the excellence of a Socrates, as compared with a fool like Sir Walter Elliott, is unmistakeably a moral one. Still, for all of its being a moral excellence, it is notwithstanding an excellence that is made evident to us in nature and from nature; it is disclosed to us directly in the very facts of nature.

And so returning now, after citing these various illustrations, to the point we sought to make in regard to the sort of conception or understanding of ethics that was traditional with philosophers of the stamp of an Aristotle or a St. Thomas. For them it is indeed from nature that we come to learn what a human being can be and ought to be, or what the standards are of human excellence, as exemplified in a Socrates, say, or as contrasted with the sort of folly, or shortcoming, or even downright evil that one can see manifested in such ones as Sir Walter Elliott or more seriously in a Hamlet or an Othello or a Macbeth or a Richard Nixon, etc. In other words, it is no less than through the study of being and of nature that we come to learn what as human beings we ought to do and be, what our obligations are as human beings, and what we need to make of ourselves, what our duties and rights are, and, in this sense, what it is that our very nature as men requires of us, as well as the various mistakes and follies and degradations that that same nature warns us against. Here, indeed, is the key to that very "natural-law philosophy" that we have so often heard ascribed to Aristotle and to St. Thomas, and in terms of which we can now come to understand what our natural end or goal, our natural standard of achievement, must needs be, simply in so far as we are human beings, and thus what it is that is naturally required of us, and what is our natural responsibility to try to be and become—, as well as, on the other hand to avoid being and becoming. And so from this there begins to emerge the whole panoply of our rights and duties.

Abandonment of Natural Law Ethics

And so returning once again to the situation of contemporary philosophy, is it not immediately apparent that unlike the so-called natural-law philosophy of Aristotle and St.

Thomas, there is literally nobody—and I mean literally nobody—in today's philosophical establishment, who would ever think of appealing to nature or to natural law in support of any kind of moral judgment—i.e. in support of what one takes to be right or wrong, or of what one holds to be our moral obligations as human beings, or of what it is that as human beings we should live for, what the good life for a man is. No, contemporary philosophers are disposed, very nearly unanimously, to laugh anything like so-called "natural law" right out of court. "Why," they would say, "it is simply ridiculous to suppose that nature can ever teach anybody anything about morals! And what is all of this naive talk about moral laws being ultimately nothing if not simply natural laws, or at least based on natural laws? Natural laws do no more than specify how human beings, simply as beings of nature, actually do act,—i.e. what the natural forces are that impinge upon them, causing them to act in this way or that. In contrast, moral laws are supposed to specify, not how men do act, but how they ought to act. Nor is there any possible way in which from a mere study of nature, and hence of what natural beings, including human beings, just do do naturally one can ever draw any inferences as to what men ought to do, or what we hold it to be incumbent upon them to do morally. In short, the study of nature can only inform us of what is the case, whereas the study of morals is supposed to inform us of what ought to be the case."

So speaks the contemporary moral philosopher! But now I ask you, "Does not the contemporary philosopher speak in accents that are passing strange, when he speaks like this?" For have we not just seen how thinkers like Aristotle and St. Thomas thought it to be nothing if not patently evident and obvious that the natural was indeed the basis of the moral,— yes, that the study of morals and ethics was itself nothing if not the study of so-called natural law? For the matter of that, would not Aquinas, for example, have gone even further and have been the first to insist that, apart from revelation, we human beings just have no other possible means of learning about morals and ethics, or of learning what our rights and duties are, save through the study of nature and of natural law? Consequently, may we not imagine either Aristotle or St. Thomas continuing right along in the same vein and saying that it is little wonder that contemporary moral philosophy is in the parlous state it is, considering that, as the basis of morality, our present-day moral philosophers are now just beginning to realize that they have thereby deprived morals or ethics, not so much of its very birthright, but even of its very claim to being? Little wonder that, with such presuppositions, ethics should thereby have been reduced to little more than the pursuit of the will-to-power.

The Choice Confronting Contemporary Ethics

Yes, even the contemporary philosopher, Alasdair MacIntyre, whom we have already cited as being one of the few who have seen the handwriting on the wall for contemporary moral philosophy, has come right out and forthrightly entitled one of the chapters of his book—the book bearing the somewhat curious title *After Virtue*—this key chapter he has entitled, "Nietzsche or Aristotle?" And what does MacIntyre imply by that title, if not that modern moral philosophy, even if it be scarcely yet aware of the fact, has really come now to its moment of truth, or, to use a rather better metaphor, to a decisive parting of the ways: either contemporary philosophers will have to realize that their entire enterprise of ethics and moral philosophy is reducible to nothing more than propaganda and the pursuit of the will to power; or they must recognize that the only other alternative open to them is to return once again to the more traditional conception of ethics, be it that of Aristotle or St. Thomas, in which the business of ethics is understood as being nothing if not the investigation of nature and of natural law.

Very well, then, why don't we but confront our generally over-confident contemporary moral philosophers with the somewhat scornful challenge: "Why don't you well-placed and highly-placed contemporary moral philosophers see the light that MacIntyre is trying to shine in your eyes, and why aren't you more ready and even eager to accept MacIntyre's proposed alternative of returning to Aristotle and to natural law, as being the only salvation for contemporary ethics?"

Alas, the business, though, is not quite so easy as all that for our contemporary philosophers. Nor does it seem to me that even MacIntyre has a proper understanding of what exactly the problems are of contemporary philosophers, if their only salvation be to return ethics once more to its one and only basis and foundation, viz. nature and natural law. Already, we have noted just in passing that the apparent reason contemporary philosophers seem to be so turned off of any notion of associating ethics with the study of nature and of natural law is that in their eyes what we call nature or the natural world, or what Aristotle, if you like, called *physis* or physics— that this is nothing if not a veritable wasteland, so far as morals and ethics are concerned. For how can anyone hope to find out anything about human rights and duties, for instance, from any study of nature and the natural world? "Just show us," we can imagine moral philosophers saying, "any duty or moral obligation that can in any wise just be read off the face of nature, or, for that matter, be dug out of the depths of nature, either! We'd just like to see one - 'Come, shepherd, instance!' "

Take, for example, just about any law of nature—yes, even take so very simple a law as "Water seeks its own level." Now suppose this to be a truth about nature, and that water does indeed seek its own level, can we say of this fact of nature either that it is really somehow quite commendable of water that it should thus seek its own level, or, as the opposite of this, that it is exceedingly unfortunate and most reprehensible of water that it thus go always hankering after its own level? "Naughty, naughty, water, you really should not do that, you know!"—clearly this kind of talk is patently ridiculous. For nature as we know it—which is to say nature, as we have come to be familiar with it through modern natural science—is totally and radically, as one might say, virtue-blind, or value-blind, or morally-blind.

The Resulting Ethics of Self-Interest

And so our contemporary moral philosopher is going to say to us—and doubtless, say to MacIntyre as well, who, after all, is one of their own kind—"You see, there is no possible way that nature can be made the basis for ethics, for nature is completely amoral, with the result that any attempt at trying to find, or to extract, norms from nature will be but a clear case of trying to derive an "ought" from an "is."

Likewise, and on the other hand, can we not begin to appreciate a little better just what modern moral philosophers have been reduced to trying to do, considering that they thought they could no longer base morals and ethics on nature or on the facts? Indeed, just put yourself in the place of someone—just anyone—who poses to himself the basic moral questions as to what he should do, how he should order his life, how conduct himself, etc. Putting now such questions to yourself, and assuming that you knew you could get no possible help in answering these questions by turning to nature, or by looking to the facts, or by relying in any way upon your experience of the world and of reality—would not then your answers possibly be more or less along Hobbesian lines? For suppose yourself to feel fully assured that there just were no natural restrictions of a moral kind on anything that you might simply fancy doing, or feel inclined to do. In other words, suppose it just is not to be imagined that there are any moral guidelines, inscribed anywhere on the face of nature, or even in the depths of nature, for that matter—guidelines, that is to say, that could in any wise be thought of as giving you instruction as to what your proper rights and duties as a human being might be. Given such a situation and such a context, would you not then feel that you were free just to do as you please, to pursue your own interests and inclinations wherever and to whatever courses of action they might lead? Indeed, I would wonder if it be not really some such basic consideration as this that lies directly at the root of all hedonistic or interest theories of ethics—theories that now-a-days tend to go by the name of *teleological* ethical theories. For is not the underlying principle of all such theories a principle to the effect that any individual's conduct of his life is to be determined simply in the light of what his particular purposes and preferences and interests and goals in life might happen to be?

Fine! Given such a presiding conviction that moral requirements and obligations have no basis or status in nature or in fact at all, then it would seem that there would be no reason why you shouldn't just do as you please. The only trouble is that simply doing as you please is not anything to which any moral worth or value could ever be attached at all. For that matter, one cannot even say that one is in any sense morally justified or warranted in simply doing what one happens to want to do. For what possible justification could there be for saying that it is only right that one should just do as one likes? True, on the assumption that there are no grounds for morality in nature, it will no doubt follow that there is then no sort of moral prohibition against doing as you please; but at the same time and by the same token, there is no positive moral warrant and justification for supposing you to have any kind of positive right to do as you please either.

A Basic Inconsistency

And right here is where, as it would seem, we could locate almost the exact point at which a basic inconsistency inserts itself into nearly all contemporary moral theories of a so-called teleological type. For just consider any one of the current varieties of utilitarianism—for these, of course, are the most typical examples in the present day of a teleological type of ethics. Invariably, such Utilitarian theories start off by counselling the individual to this effect: in life you need only do as you please, you need only concern yourself with maximizing your own interests, your own pleasures, your own happiness, and minimizing your pains and sufferings and disadvantages. But then, having made this point, the Utilitarian moralist suddenly makes a curious twist or—yes, even a dubious kind of swerve: from telling the individual that he need worry about nothing save only maximizing his own interests and pleasures, he now starts talking about the obligation any individual is under to work for the greatest good or the greatest happiness of the greatest number.

But just where did such an obligation come from? Surely, this must bring up sharp the poor, innocent, and unsuspecting counsellee of the Utilitarian moralist. For will he not think that he has somehow been had? "But I thought I was being told that in life I did not have to worry about anything but maximizing my own interests and my own happiness. And now you tell me that I must also worry about the interests and happiness of others, no less than my own. In fact, it is held to be nothing if not my moral duty and obligation to work for the greatest happiness of the greatest number! But how and where and on what basis did such a duty to others ever get smuggled into the picture? Indeed, I feel as if I were only being led down the garden path, being told first that the only thing I need concern myself with in life is my own happiness and my own well-being, and then, suddenly and before I know it, I end up being told that I have to concern myself with the happiness of others no less than my own. Truly, I feel as if I really had been had in all of this Utilitarian stuff!"

From Teleology to Deontology

And so the poor fellow has indeed been had! For what the Utilitarian moralist has done has been to slip from what might be called an entirely "duty-free" teleological account of

human living, as if that involved only pursuing one's own interests and purposes, to a radically different account of the
business of living, which in effect transforms one's whole
ethical theory from being a teleological one to being a deontological one. Oh, it's true we are all familiar with how the
Utilitarians, and the various species of ethical teleologists
who are like them, have struggled manfully, not to say even
sophistically, to try to justify this surreptitious smuggling of a
deontological note into what is otherwise a supposedly pure
and non-obligatory type of hedonism or interest-theory. John
Stuart Mill, for example, at least gave an appearance of committing a sort of fallacy of composition when he seemed to
argue that just as the individual's happiness is the aim of each
individual taken separately, so the general happiness must
therefore be the aim of all individuals taken collectively.

Likewise, and more recently, R. M. Hare has tried to in-
voke the so-called Principle of Universalizability as a way of
showing how on Utilitarian grounds an individual is supposedly committed not just to pursuing his own interests, but the
interests of others as well. However, we will not take time to
show in detail just how this invocation of the Principle of
Universalizability just will not do the trick of turning a mere
ethical teleology into a deontology. Suffice it only to say that
while there is nothing wrong with the so-called Principle of
Universalizability itself, there is much that is wrong with supposing that the Principle of Universalizability has an applica-
bility in the instant case at all: Just because I have a concern
to pursue my own interests, it simply does not follow that out
of that fact alone it can ever be demonstrated that I have an
obligation to be concerned with the interests of others no less
than with my own.

But, then, if so-called teleological theories of ethics, such
as are fashionable in the present day, can thus be shown to be
quite bankrupt, and hence radically and totally indefensible as
ethical theories, then what about the supposedly contrasting
deontological theories that are no less fashionable today, and

that, all of them, pretty much would trace their origins right back to Immanuel Kant? For the point of any contemporary deontological theory of ethics in the present day is just that any such theory takes so-called duties and obligations to be morally and ethically ultimate. That is to say, instead of supposing that the reason a person ought to do thus and so is only because by that means alone can he ever attain some end or purpose that he happens to have, a deontological theory holds that in the final analysis "oughts" are ultimate, and are not to be understood in terms of any prior ends or purposes or interests or whatever. In other words, in the final analysis it is never that we ought to do so and so, because we want something else; rather it is that we ought to do so and so, because we ought—and that's that! It is just as Kant said: categorical imperatives have an ultimate priority over mere hypothetical imperatives.

Very well, then, but what is the basis for these categorical oughts that the deontologists insist that we are bound by? For remember that, just as with the present-day teleologists, so also the present-day deontologists are convinced that there can be no appeal to nature or to natural law as somehow providing a basis for such categorical imperatives, or for that matter for moral requirements of any kind that might supposedly be binding upon us.

No, for all such appeals to nature and to natural law, as presumably providing a basis and justification for morality are simply ruled out, as we have seen,—and this for the reason that deontological thinkers, just like all other thinkers in the modern world, take it to be quite beyond question that nature, such as it is disclosed to be by modern natural science, is of absolutely no relevance for morality at all: nature and the laws of nature are totally and radically amoral, that's all! Or to put it a bit differently: nature is no less indifferent to the most atrocious crimes, than it is to the most resplendent examples of virtue and of heroism; the one sort of behavior can no more be said to be in violation of any dictates of nature, than the other can be said to be in accord with any natural dictates or natural laws. And that's that!

Is There a Ground for Duty?

But then, the question presses even more: what possible justification can be given for the supposed duties and obligations that are incumbent upon us? Thus for instance, as an American citizen, I am aware that under the fifth and the fourteenth amendments to the constitution, no one may be deprived of life, liberty, or property without due process of law. But why not? Why may I not deprive my neighbor of his liberty and his property, if I am able to and can get away with it? Why is that wrong? Oh, it's true that within the jurisdiction of the U.S., I may—hopefully I will—fall afoul of the law, if I deprive someone of his life or his liberty or his property. But the mere legal wrongs in such instances supposedly have underpinnings in certain moral wrongs. Accordingly, the question that we are now pressing is: Just why and how and on what grounds can it be said to be morally wrong that I deprive my neighbor of his life or liberty or property?

Or again, take Kant's own celebrated categorical imperative: So act that you can always will that the maxim of your action should be a universal law; or again, so act as to treat human nature, whether in your own person or in that of another, always as an end and never merely as a means. But again, suppose one asks, Why shouldn't I treat my neighbor merely as a means to my own interests and purposes? What's wrong with that?

Well, as we all know, Kant would respond to such a challenge by saying that such conduct, while it by no means can be said to violate any natural laws, nevertheless can be said to lead anyone indulging in such conduct into serious inconsistency and even self-contradiction. To which the answer is: "Sorry, but that is too farfetched to be in any way credible. Indeed, when one scrutinizes Kant's own examples and arguments designed to show how conduct that is in ruthless disregard of one's neighbors' interests must necessarily lead the perpetrator of such conduct into inconsistency and contradiction, one finds that the arguments and examples just will not hold up. They just don't bear scrutiny for an instant."

Accordingly, many deontologists on the contemporary scene, realizing that Kant's arguments in support of his categorical imperatives just are not defensible—as if the violation of such imperatives would lead to inconsistency—these deontologists have used a rather different device in support of the supposed categorical "oughts" that are held to be binding upon us. For they would say that human beings are able simply to "intuit" that certain courses of action are wrong—e.g. depriving another of his life or liberty or property. Moreover, in insisting that any moral agent is able thus to intuit such actions as being wrong, the contemporary deontologist must not be taken to mean that the moral violator can somehow see such actions to be wrong in the sense of their being found to be contrary to nature or in conflict with empirically discoverable laws of right and wrong in nature. No, for in accord with the entire spirit of present-day ethics, the ethical intuitionist must not just admit, but insist, that a knowledge of nature can teach one nothing whatever about right and wrong. Instead, we intuit certain things as being right, and others as being wrong, in the sense that we just intuit them to be so, period.

Surely, though, any such appeal to a supposed direct moral insight or intuition will never do! For that matter, it only begs the question. After all, what that question was was a question of how to make a cogent rejoinder to someone who just doesn't see that there might be anything wrong with depriving another of his life or his liberty or his property. For such a moral scoff-law would in effect be asking: "Just show me what's wrong with such conduct!" To this kind of a challenge, however, one scarcely can be said to make a cogent rejoinder merely by saying, "Oh, but my good man, can't you just 'see' or 'intuit' that such behavior toward another is wrong and ought not to be." In other words, the mere appeal

to intuition in justification of moral obligations and imperatives comes off as nothing if not an exercise in downright
arbitrariness!

II

And with that, then, does not the predicament of contemporary ethics and moral philosophy become crystal clear?
If the modern philosopher repudiates nature and natural law
as providing a basis and grounding for morals and ethics, then
all moral rules and prescriptions regarding right and wrong,
good and bad, etc., turn out to be wholly without foundation;
on the other hand, if the present-day moral philosopher
should consider, even for so much as an instant, the possibility
of our once more looking to nature and to natural law as
possibly providing us with a source of genuine moral knowledge, there then tends to be borne in upon him the seeming
massive testimony of modern natural science, all of it being,
apparently, in outright denial of the very possibility of any
such alternative. For has it not become the consensus alike of
scientists, and of just about everybody else in today's world—
that nothing—and I mean nothing!—is ever discoverable in
nature and the natural world that will ever give us so much
as a clue, much less any genuine knowledge, as to the differ-
ences between right and wrong, or as to what our rights and
duties as human persons might ever be? Accordingly, the dilemma that MacIntyre would pose for our moral philosophers—
as if the choice were simply one of going either with Nietzsche
or Aristotle—may be all very well. The problem, though, is,
How is one ever to meet such a dilemma? Certainly, if you
will, we all of us—or at least most of us—would presumably not
want to accept the Nietzschean alternative of considering the
pursuit of moral philosophy as being but an exercise in the will
to power. On the other hand, as modern moral philosophers
we surely can no longer go the way of Aristotle and St.
Thomas of trying to ground ethics in nature and natural law.

For here again it is precisely the testimony of modern natural science that renders the choice of such an alternative not just unwarranted, but little better than blatantly obscurantist. So what to do?

Nature, a Moral Wasteland to Present Philosophers. Why?

Well, if I am not mistaken, there unfortunately is no one among modern moral philosophers who really seems to know very much what to do under the circumstances. No, not even MacIntyre; for while he has been very acute in posing his dilemma for modern moral philosophers, he has been regrettably vague and imprecise, and maybe even evasive, as to how modern moral philosophy might be able to extricate itself from its unhappy predicament. Yet, surely, there must be some way, somehow, that someone might be able to point the way to modern moral philosophers, whereby they could find "a happy issue out of all of their afflictions."

Moreover, just by way of a beginning, why might it not be asked just why it should have been that thinkers like Aristotle and Aquinas should never have had really any difficulty with the idea that moral standards and moral distinctions were discoverable directly within nature itself, whereas modern thinkers, presumably following the lead of the modern natural scientists, would simply write off the entire order of nature as being nothing if not a total and utter moral wasteland? In a way the answer to such a question is not too far to seek. For is it not clear to everybody that the very conception and understanding of nature (and of natural law, as well), with which thinkers like Aristotle and Aquinas were operating, differed, really almost *toto caelo*, from the general notion and understanding of nature with which modern scientists operate?

Moreover, to point up these differing conceptions of nature, why do we not just briefly counterpose Descartes to Aristotle? For surely, we are all of us familiar with how for Aristotle nature and the natural world were permeated and shot through with what we might best characterize as being a pervasive teleology: tadpoles tend to develop into frogs, seeds into full grown plants, and even in purely inanimate nature— at least so Aristotle thought—heavy bodies tend toward their "natural places" at the center of the universe, just as light bodies tend naturally toward the periphery. In other words, all of the different species and kinds of things in nature have their natural ends, as well as their natural mode and manner of development ordered to such ends.

Contrast, though, Descartes. And I take it that for purposes of this discussion we can simply accept the fact that it was indeed Descartes who set the stage and provided the model for the modern scientific conception and account of nature. Moreover, what would seem to be the most striking and salient feature of this modern scientific conception of nature is that it is what one can only call a thoroughly mathematized account of nature. In fact, one could say that as his models for the types and kinds of things that there are in nature, Descartes would seem to have focused not so much upon natural species of the ordinary sort—animals, plants, insects, fish, human beings, etc. Instead, it was as if the only species he took account of were such as were modelled upon purely mathematical entities, particularly geometrical entities —circles, squares, triangles, rhomboids, chiliagons, et al.

At the same time, of course, as we all doubtless know, it was Aristotle who had pointed out long before Descartes that the species of geometrical objects are, in the very nature of the case, not subject to any natural changes or developments, in the way in which natural species are. A circle, for example, just isn't potentially a square in the way in which an acorn is potentially an oak; nor is any circle subject to any sort of natural change or development culminating in its becoming a square, in the way in which, say, an acorn changes and develops naturally into an oak tree. No, one might say that, just in its own nature, a geometrical object like a circle is completely unchanging: it's static, it's just itself, and not subject even to the slightest conceivable kind of development at all.

But, then, Aristotle goes on to point out, if geometrical objects are thus not subject to any natural changes or developments, there could of course be no such things as final causes in geometry—at least not in the sense in which final causes in the natural world are to be understood as being but the natural ends or natural culminations, or termini, of natural processes of change. In geometry, one just does not find anything of this sort at all.

Besides, if geometrical objects lack all potentialities for development, they will lack what Aristotle called material causes as well (at least in the strict sense of material causes, and not in the sense of any so-called "intelligible matter"). And without material and final causes—and indeed, not being really subject to change at all—it is clear that so far as geometrical objects are concerned, they won't be subject to any efficient or moving causes either. In fact, mathematics, Aristotle suggested, is the domain simply of formal causes, much like Plato's Forms,—a domain simply of static, eternal and unchanging essences.

Very well, suppose that this mathematical or geometrical model is now, as it was indeed by Descartes, simply read on to the face of nature. Is it not obvious that the natural world of Descartes—and since this basic Cartesian model became pretty much the standard for the whole of modern science, we can say that it has turned out to be the natural world of modern science as well—that this entire Cartesian, scientific universe now comes to be seen as a universe in which, strictly speaking, there are no changes or developments at all; instead, there are only successions of events (Descartes spoke of a constant re-creation of the universe at each moment of time). Not only that, but the scientific universe, not being a universe of changing or developing beings in any sense, will not be a universe of any teleology or of final causes either. In fact, we all know how Descartes boasted of having eliminated so-called final causation from the universe altogether.

Clearly, though, if both potentialities and final causes are eliminated from the natural world, then goodness or value

will have no kind of status in such a universe either. For recall
that Aristotle understood goodness and value pretty much in
terms of final causes: the good of anything is simply its natural
end or natural perfection. And so likewise, Aquinas tended to
understand, or even define, *bonum* or good as being simply the
actual as over against the potential, or the perfect as over
against the imperfect, or the complete as over against the incomplete. But without goodness or value anywhere in the
universe, then there can hardly be any talk of what anything
ought to do or be. For the rudimentary notion of "ought," in
any Aristotelian or Thomistic framework, must simply be the
notion of what is requisite, or what needs to be done, or what
steps have to be gone through, if a thing's natural end or final
cause is ever to be achieved.

Very well! Suppose, then, that nature and the natural
world of Aristotle and Aquinas differed from nature and the
natural world of modern science pretty much along the lines
of these respective specifications as given by Aristotle on the
one hand, and by Descartes on the other, just what are we to
do about the matter; or what can we do about the matter? For
is not the problem, particularly with respect to ethics, simply
this: if nature is teleological in its character and structure,
much as Aristotle and Aquinas thought it to be, then ethics
can once more be given a firm footing and foundation, and
not be written off as but so much charlatanry and sophistry.
And yet unhappily, the notion of nature as teleological is
something seemingly quite beyond recall, considering how the
accumulated evidence of nearly three centuries of modern
natural science would seem to have shown that it was
Descartes who was right as over against Aristotle; nature is
not, and cannot be, teleological in any way, and the scientific
evidence is there to demonstrate the fact!

Teleology Not Incompatible with the "New View of Science"

But is it? Is it true to say that the empirical findings of
science have now indeed established that nature is non-

teleological? To this question I should like, in the latter part of this paper, to give a qualified "No" by way of answer. For in suggesting that nature and the natural world perhaps need to be reckoned as being teleological after all—and this despite the seemingly intractable testimony of modern science to the contrary—I would hope that in all of this I am not being merely obscurantist. Instead, I believe that possibly I can make appeal directly to a number of recent, and, as I would see it, rather exciting, new developments in the philosophy of science, by way of trying ultimately to work around to a defense of what would seem to me to be that quite undeniable teleology that is evidenced directly in the world of nature. For what these new developments in the philosophy of science point to is certainly not to any "doing down" of science. Nor can they be in any wise taken as proving that Aristotle was simply right after all, and Descartes wrong, in their respective accounts of nature and the natural world. No, the upshot of such new developments in the philosophy of science is rather to suggest an entirely new and different way of conceiving the nature of the scientific enterprise, as if possibly it should be taken to have a quite different character from what it has so long been thought to have had—and been thought to have had even by the scientists themselves. In fact, this "new view of science," as it is now sometimes called, is a view according to which, so far from being concerned to tell us what nature is really like, based on observation and experiment, the scientist should rather be thought to be concerned with putting forward merely various pictures or hypotheses or world-views from which nature may be viewed, and in terms of which the scientist can then manipulate and get a certain purchase on the data, but without necessarily either trying or presuming to say what nature is really like in itself at all. In short, to recur to our earlier line of example and illustration, if Descartes' mathematized, and hence completely non-teleological, picturing of nature is just not to be taken as being a literally true representation of the way nature really is, but rather as but a convenient device for enabling us to better cope with the data, and so to further our better control over nature—should such be the character and import of scientific theories in the strict sense, and should we accordingly take Descartes' view of nature to be no more than a scientific theory in this strict sense, then there is no reason why nature in itself should not be thoroughly teleological in character, even though from the standpoint of the scientist, this would not be a particularly convenient way of looking at nature: it would not enable the scientist to achieve the kind of arrangement and ordering of the data such as would facilitate the kind of prediction and control over nature that the scientist, as scientist, is interested in.

Now as most of you are no doubt aware, this so-called "new view of science" can trace its origins back largely to the distinguished contemporary philosopher of science, Sir Karl Popper. And basically, what Popper's contention was was that it is a mistake to suppose that science and scientific laws really in any proper sense rest on observation and induction. Oh, it's true that, as Popper readily conceded, certain low-level scientific laws, such as that "Silver melts at 960.5 degrees C," or "Water boils at 100 degrees C"—such low-level laws are, no doubt, established by induction. Nevertheless, when we consider not so much these low-level scientific laws, as rather the great over-arching theories and hypotheses of science—e.g. Kepler's hypothesis as to the elliptical orbits of the planets, say, or Newton's laws of motion—it is ridiculous, Popper insists, to suppose that these latter are in any way based on any kind of observation or induction. For instance, Kepler did not go out and observe that several of the planets did in fact move in elliptical, and not in circular orbits, as had formerly been supposed, and then conclude from this that all planets move in elliptical orbits. That's absurd! Likewise, Newton's law that a body not acted upon by an external force continues indefinitely in motion or at rest—surely, this law was not arrived at by observing first several bodies not to be acted upon by external forces, and yet continuing on indefinitely in motion or at rest, and then generalizing from this that all bodies not acted upon by external forces must so behave.

And so Popper asks, How does the scientist arrive at these high level laws and theories? Popper's answer is: He simply invents them, dreams them up, makes them up out of whole cloth, as it were. Indeed, Popper even stresses the fact that the devising and projecting of scientific hypotheses and theories by the great geniuses of science—the Keplers, the Newtons, the Einsteins—so far from being based on any laborious experimentation and observation, is like nothing so much as artistic creation—thinking up a symphony, conceiving a great work of art, etc. All the same, the question arises: But if scientific hypotheses and theories are not really derived from experience and observation at all, if they are no more than dreamed up and invented, then on what basis are they accepted? How, in other words, does a really successful hypothesis come actually to be accepted and established, as compared, say, with the mere dreams or contrivances of some lunatic?

To such a question, Popper's own answer was that while one may not suppose that hypotheses ever come to be verified in experience—after all, that would be comparable to induction—, it is nonetheless only right and proper to recognize that scientific hypotheses do need to be tested in the light of at least some kind of experience, albeit in a somewhat backhanded way. Accordingly, Popper insists that the test has to be conceived of as being one of falsification, rather than of verification. The business of the scientist, therefore, is not one of discovering explanatory causes and principles in the facts, so much as it is a matter of trying to see whether, once one has dreamed up a hypothesis, or simply made it up out of whole cloth, it is possible then to find any contrary or falsifying evidence in the facts of observation.

The only trouble is that as any number of Popper's successors—philosophers of science like the famous Thomas Kuhn—have pointed out, there is just no way in which falsifying evidence with respect to a hypothesis can ever be made to be truly decisive and conclusive. After all, to take but a single trivial example, say Boyle's law to the effect that the pressure and volume of a gas will be found to vary inversely. Suppose that on a particular occasion the pressure and volume do not vary inversely, the chemist does not say that the law has been falsified; instead, he looks for some disturbing factors—say, atmospheric pressure—that will account for the deviations from the predicted variation in the gas. Or to use a somewhat more trivial example, I might cite the example which Prof. C. I. Lewis sometimes used in his Harvard philosophy classes of some 50 years ago. "After all," Lewis said in effect, "there is no reason why astronomers today should not continue to use the old Ptolemaic system in astronomy, rather than the newer systems of Copernicus and Kepler, should they but choose to do so. The only trouble would be that they would then have to make so many *ad hoc* adjustments in the Ptolemaic system—such as adding epicycles upon epicycles—that the human mind would simply collapse in the face of the complicated mathematics involved." To all of which one might be tempted to add today that, when Lewis used such an illustration, it was long before the invention and use of computers!

Very well, then, but if scientific laws and theories are thus not subject to any real test by experience—i.e. they are subject neither to verification nor even to any decisive falsification by the empirical evidence—what possible reason is there for our ever accepting any scientific theory or hypothesis, as over against some other or opposite theory? This time the answer turns out to be that we accept a scientific theory, not on the basis of any sort of evidence of its truth, but only on the basis of purely pragmatic considerations, according to which it would seem to be to our advantage simply to believe the hypothesis to be true. That is to say, the hypothesis that wins out is merely the one that seems to work better, or that serves our purposes better, with the result that whether we view nature in one way rather than another turns out to be largely a matter of choice and preference.

And with this, oddly enough, we find that this newly popular way of understanding science and scientific theory comes around to a view of knowledge that was made celebrated by Immanuel Kant in the late 18th century. For Kant, despairing of our ever being able, as he put it, to bring our ideas and our theories into conformity with the facts, suggested instead that we might begin to try to bring the facts into conformity with our ideas and our theories. And how is this possible? Well, if we but recognize that perhaps our ideas and theories and views of reality or of nature need not be taken, and should not be taken, as being in any way descriptions or reflections of the facts, as these really are in themselves, but only as our ways of viewing the facts, or the perspectives from which we view them, then obviously it will turn out that the facts as we know them must necessarily conform to our ideas and modes of viewing them. And as to what reality and the facts are like just in themselves—well, that is something that we just don't know about and can't know about, since the facts as we know them must always be seen through the medium of our particular theories and ideas that we employ simply as a way of looking at the facts. To use but a crude example, if I wear jaundiced glasses, then everything that I see will appear to me to be yellow. Of course, the things that I thus see are not necessarily yellow in themselves; and yet never will I be able to see them as anything other than yellow, so long as I never take off the glasses!

Consider, then, what the consequences are of this "new view of science," as we have been calling it, once it comes to be closely associated with the standard Kantian view of knowledge generally. Clearly, the consequence will be that science, supposing that it relies upon the Popperian method of hypothesis, does not and cannot tell us what the world of nature is really like in itself. Instead, science can do no more than inform us of what nature and the world of nature *appear* to be like, when seen through the medium of the particular scientific theory or hypothesis that we happen to be using or operating with at the time. But never by any such method of hypothesis can we hope to know what nature or the world is really like in itself at all.

Accordingly, recalling the Cartesian view of nature as completely mathematized and non-teleological, we now find ourselves constrained to recognize that such a Cartesian view of nature does not tell us the way nature really is at all. No, it is merely a way of looking at nature, or a kind of conceptual construct that we ourselves imposed upon nature from the outside, and in terms of which we come to view both nature and all of the events and happenings that take place within nature. Hence once Descartes' theory or account of nature comes to be treated as but a kind of scientific hypothesis, then it turns out to be no more than a device for making nature appear to us a certain way—i.e. as entirely devoid of any final causes or purposive or developmental change. But of course, just because that is the way nature must appear to us to be, once we put on Cartesian glasses, it certainly does not necessarily follow that there really are no natural ends or final causes in nature at all. No, it's just that the Cartesian hypothesis makes things appear that way to us.

But, then, you will ask: on this new view of science—a view which has so many overtones of Kantian transcendental philosophy—, is there no way in which scientists, or human beings generally, might change their theories or hypotheses for looking at the world, thus bringing in an entirely new set of hypotheses for viewing nature or reality? And to this, the answer is that of course there is. In fact, the variety of our possible hypotheses and world-views, if we choose to call them that, are as limitless as is the capacity of our creative imaginations for dreaming up such hypotheses originally and in the first place. Indeed, as we all know, the operative hypotheses in modern physics, since its inception in the seventeenth century, have been anything but fixed and unchanging—Descartes, Leibniz, Newton, Einstein, the quantum theorists—have all offered new and often quite strikingly different hypotheses from which to view the world.

Moreover, since, on the new view of science, the change from one scientific theory or world-view to another can never be based on evidence in any strict sense—neither falsifying evidence of old views nor a verifying evidence of new ones— the change from one way of looking at the world to another is, as we might say, completely wide-open. Accordingly, it can be no more than merely pragmatic considerations that determine our preferences for one theory or world-view as over against another. Hence if there are but sufficient pragmatic considerations in support of them, there is no reason why we might not come to prefer just about any imaginable world-view, say, that of the ancient Greek gods, or maybe one concocted from the fantasies of William Blake, or perhaps a creation of some of the wilder speculations of the ancient Gnostics. In short, so far as hypotheses and world-views are concerned, the field is absolutely wide-open!

Yes, why do we not cite in evidence at this point the well-known, even if perhaps somewhat puckish, pronouncements of W. V. Quine on the relative merits of a world consisting of physical objects in the modern scientific sense, as contrasted with a world peopled by the ancient Greek gods of Olympus:

> As an empiricist I continue to think of the conceptual scheme of science as a tool, ultimately, for predicting future experience in the light of past experience. Physical objects are conceptually imported into the situation as convenient intermediaries—not by definition in terms of experience, but simply as irreducible posits comparable, epistemologically, to the gods of Homer. For my part I do, qua lay physicist, believe in physical objects and not in Homer's gods; and I consider it a scientific error to believe otherwise. But in point of epistemological footing the physical objects and the gods differ only in degree and not in kind. Both sorts of entities enter our conception only as cultural posits. The myth of physical objects is epistemologically superior to most in that it has proved more efficacious than other myths as a device for working a manageable structure into the flux of experience. (W. V. Quine, *From a Logical Point of View*, p. 44)

Nor is Quine's example the only one that we might cite in this connection. For of late, there have been others besides Quine —Paul Feyerabend, Richard Rorty, Robert Nozick, to name

but a few, more or less randomly chosen—who have been hint-
ing, albeit sometimes a bit gingerly, that, much as we earlier
found MacIntyre to be suggesting that since contemporary
ethical theories would appear to have no basis in the facts or
in any sort of reliable empirical evidence, and that therefore
the pursuit of ethics reflects nothing more than the exercise
of a Nietzschean kind of will to power, so also now it begins
to appear that as regards scientific hypotheses and world-views
generally, since there would seem to be no kind of empirical
evidence that can be derived from the facts by way of verifying
or falsifying them, the consequence would appear almost inescapable that all science and all philosophy, and not just
moral philosophy, begins now to take on the guise of being little more than a sort of ruthless Nietzschean exercise of the will
to power.

Oh, but wait a minute! And happily we can wait a minute, for before we allow ourselves to be swept away in all of
these Nietzschean eddies, now not just with respect to contemporary moral philosophy, but with respect to contemporary philosophy generally, we should draw ourselves up sharp
and remind ourselves of what that earlier question and challenge of ours was that got us into all of this. It was simply the
question of whether there might be any way in which we
might return morals and ethics to a firm footing in nature and
in natural law, simply by means of rehabilitating something
like the ancient Aristotelian and Thomistic view of nature as
being teleological. Moreover, what proved to be the principal
roadblock obstructing any such return to a teleological view
of nature was just the fact that such a view of nature seemed
to be thoroughly and radically incompatible with the modern
scientific and Cartesian view of nature from which any and
every vestige of teleology would appear to be excluded.

The New View of Science Opens the Door to a Nature-Based Ethics

Now, however, it begins to appear that any and all scientific views of nature, Cartesian or otherwise, so far from ex-

cluding a teleological account of nature, are really not competitors of a natural teleology at all. No, for on "the new view of science," it turns out that science does not and should not even pretend to be an account of the way the world really is. Instead, all scientific theories and hypotheses are but so many ways of rigging things in such ways as to make nature appear as being of a certain character—say non-teleological—when that may not be the way nature and the world really are at all. Hence there is just no incompatibility between nature's appearing to be non-teleological from the point of view of the scientist, and at the same time being really teleological in fact and in itself—this last being the way it is recognized to be by the philosopher.

Oh, but you will say, why is not that more or less Aristotelian account of nature and of natural ends and final causes, such as we sketched it out earlier, itself but a kind of hypothesis and world-view, and hence not anything that can claim to be an account of nature as it really is, any more than this can be claimed by any scientific view? But no, for this rejoinder is easily answerable. Remember that the basis on which it was earlier argued that science treats only of appearances and not of reality was that modern science relies basically on the method of hypothesis. This, indeed, has been the root contention of the new view of science.

However, while such a view of science may be entirely defensible, so far as science is concerned, it is not accurate as a description of philosophy—at least not of Aristotelian or Thomistic philosophy. For it is not by any method of hypothesis that Aristotle determined that real changes go on in nature. No, that things change is, for Aristotle, a fact of observation, and not any mere hypothesis. Not only that, but Aristotle would surely insist that, so far from being a hypothesis, it is again but an obvious fact that any and all things that undergo change—you and I, plants and animals, the temperature in this room, the table on which I am writing—that these are all things that must be subject to change, just in the sense that they could not change unless they were able to change, or unless, as an Aristotelian would say, they had a potentiality for becoming other and different. The air in the room, for example, is now hot—yes, full of hot air, if you will—and yet it can be cooled. The acorn is not an oak tree, but it is potentially one. The foetus is in certain respects not fully human, but it is potentially so. All of you readers are now bored, but you might have been entertained, etc., etc.

Moreover, be it noted also that when we all of us recognize that there just are potentialities in things—that such potentialities are real facts of nature, and not mere hypotheses, in the sense of somewhat jaundiced ways of looking at nature—recognizing this much, we thereby also recognize that the fact of there being such potentialities in things of the world means that in nature things are nearly always not all that they might be or could be. Yes, are not all of you saying at this very moment that this paper is certainly not all that it might have been? Not only that, but in saying that it is not all that it might have been, you are also and at the same time painfully conscious of the fact that it is not all that it should have been either! Nor is even that all. For while we are about it, why not recall as well the earlier quoted characterization of Sir Walter Elliott? Would not one say that, Sir Walter being the ass that he was, he just was not all that he might have been, or could have been, and so ought to have been simply as a human being? In other words, Sir Walter was patently and palpably someone who simply did not live up to his potentialities as a human person.

And now see, what have we here! For in just this brief and cursory—yes, even almost puerile—account that we have just been giving of certain simple and elementary facts of nature—facts that really are facts of nature and no mere functions of some hypothesis or way of looking at nature—just consider what we have found: we have found that there are real changes that do take place in nature; that the things that change really do have various capacities and potentialities; that these conditions of potentiality may be contrasted with conditions of actuality; that these actualities with respect to which things are only in potency really do represent kinds of standards of perfection in nature—i.e. they represent what things might be and could be, what they are thus aimed at being, or are ordered to being, simply by nature, if you will.

And so with the recognition of such facts of nature as involving no less than natural ends, and natural standards of perfection, may we not also be said thus to have recognized, at least by implication, certain natural "oughts"—that is to say what people and things ought to be, simply by virtue of their very natures. The tree, as we say, ought to be full grown and not merely sickly and stunted in its growth. Or again, given their potentialities and capacities as human beings, both Sir Walter Elliott and poor Henry Veatch ought to be far better men than they either were or are. In other words, so far from "oughts"—yes even moral "oughts"—and with "oughts" all of the other paraphernalia of morality as well—so far from such "oughts" being extrinsic to nature, they are right there to be discovered within nature and in the facts of nature.

Accordingly, then, be it noted that none of this list of things that we have hastily enumerated as being features and characteristics of the natural world—none of these represents any mere hypothesis which has been somehow dreamed up to "explain" otherwise unintelligible phenomena and data in nature. No, they are nothing if not directly observable features of nature itself. In this sense they are simply evident from observation and induction. Nor in any wise can one say that one has here to do with any kind of unverifiable and unfalsifiable hypotheses. Instead, it is the facts of nature themselves that are here being disclosed, and as facts of nature they are no less than the basis for the facts of ethics as well.

What, then, may we say in conclusion as regards the dilemma MacIntyre poses for contemporary moral philosophy: either Nietzsche or Aristotle? Well, if one remains within the constrictions of contemporary philosophy, it would seem that the horrendous Nietzschean alternative becomes almost inescapable: if not only ethics, but science and philosophy as well, cannot claim to be based on the facts of nature and being, then theirs cannot be a legitimate exercise of knowledge at all, but only of the will-to-power. On the other hand, in the light of what we have now been saying, there is a way, after all, in which a true philosophy of nature can be rehabilitated, and with it a true ethics and moral philosophy as well. Yes, if that way be followed, then I see no reason why a revived Aristotelian and Thomistic philosophy might not indeed be able to point the way to a largely bankrupt contemporary philosophy, so that from its present parlous state, it may now find a happy issue out of all its afflictions!

Center for Thomistic Studies
University of St. Thomas

Voluntariness and the Insanity Plea

Vernon J. Bourke

Current interest in the Hinckley case has elicited a number of proposals to abolish or modify the use of the insanity
plea in U.S. courts of law. To some people it appears that
guilty criminals are abusing this type of defense. To others it
seems that some changes should be made in our present views
on insanity. It is not reassuring to see several psychiatrists
testify that an accused person was of unsound mind at the time
of a given action—and then to witness an equal number of experts declare that this person was not insane at that time.

The insanity plea has had a long history in Anglo-
American legal affairs.[1] British courts provided us with the
famous M'Naghten Rule (from an 1843 case) which states that
decisions regarding insanity must be based on "whether at the
time of the committing of the act, the party accused was labor-
ing under such a defect of reason from disease of the mind as
not to know the nature and quality of the act he was doing,
or if he did know it, that he did not know he was doing what
was wrong." Noteworthy in this test is the use of "disease" in
reference to the mind and the suggestion that this defect may
be temporary, that is, present "at the time of the committing
of the act." We may also note that this rule stresses the failure
to know something: it emphasizes the cognitive element in
alleged insanity. Three centuries earlier in the English courts
the William Lambard case had declared that the determination of lunacy was proper when a person "cannot be said to

45

have any understanding will." This decision made in 1582 used language ("understanding" and "will") that had a definite meaning in those days, because Scholastic philosophy was still being taught in British universities and was being used to some extent in popular political tracts. Where the M'Naghten rule speaks of "mind," the earlier case used the more precise phrase "understanding will." Many efforts have since been made to improve the M'Naghten rule. One great difficulty in setting up such a norm lies in the lack of a standard and well understood set of psychological terms whose meaning may be grasped even by not too well educated members of a jury. In 1966 (in the Freeman case) Judge Irving R. Kaufman enunciated the following rule which has been widely adopted in U.S. courts: "a person is not responsible for criminal conduct if at the time of such conduct as a result of mental disease or defect he lacks substantial capacity either to appreciate the wrongfulness of his conduct or to conform his conduct to the requirements of law."

This rule uses rather simple and non-technical language but it relies on the central concept of "mental disease or defect." Judge Kaufman was well aware of the obscurity of this phrase. Quite rightly he remarks that institutions for the insane are filled with people who are not lacking in cognitive ability. Most have problems that seem to arise from emotional disorders. This is well illustrated by the famous story of the driver who has a flat tire in front of an institution for the insane. While changing his tire the wheel nuts roll into a storm sewer and the driver can't attach his spare. An inmate peering through the fence suggests that he remove one nut from each of the other three wheels and use them until he can reach a service station. In delighted surprise the driver accepts the suggestion but asks: "if you're that smart what are you doing in there?" The inmate replies: "I may be crazy but I'm not dumb!" Nothing indicates better the plurality of factors in consciousness. There is not one kind of mental illness; many things may go wrong within human experiences of knowing, willing and feeling.

The very experts who presume to diagnose and treat various mental defects are notoriously unreliable as witnesses. Juries may be, and frequently are, instructed that they are free to ignore the opinions offered in court by psychiatrists but how is the ordinary man or woman serving on a jury (or even the ordinary court official) to decide whether the mental condition of the accused was "diseased" at the time of the alleged crime which may have occurred two or three years prior to the trial? May I say immediately that I do not think the solution to such problems lies in the abolition of the insanity plea? In some cases the defendant has been involved in a bodily action that is illegal but which the defendant has not engaged in with what lawyers call a *mens rea* (guilty mind). It is not my present purpose to develop further the legal ramifications of this problem. The foregoing is but a prologue to the philosophical point that I wish to make. That is the contention that some of the features of Thomas Aquinas' analysis of voluntariness could provide us with the analytic factors needed by both experts and ordinary people faced with the problem of determining when and whether a mind is unsound. As we shall see, these factors are fourfold: 1) *cognitive*, that is, having to do with defects in knowledge; 2) *volitional*, in the sense of willing defectively or failing to will; 3) *emotional*, that is, pertaining to some affective experience that impedes or prevents conformity with good practical judgment; and 4) *habitual*, in the sense of acquired and rather permanent dispositions that may in some instances diminish personal responsibility for a given extra-mental action. To deal clearly with these four factors some commonly shared understanding of the terms used to describe conditions of consciousness is necessary. It would be very helpful if psychologists, psychiatrists, philosophers, and others working in the mental health field could settle on a standard and adequate terminology. Eventually a sufficient grasp of such a language of psychic experience might develop in the general public, so that people on all levels of education would understand at least the basic notions involved in an appraisal of mental stability.

AQUINAS' ANALYSIS OF VOLUNTARINESS

In the psychology of Thomas Aquinas a radical distinction is made between cognition and appetition.[2] To know is
to receive and judge information from various kinds of objects;
but to love, desire, enjoy—or dislike, reject, suffer sorrow—is
to respond affectively to such known objects. In the order of
cognition, the movement is from outside the mind to inside
consciousness; but the movement of appetition is in the opposite direction, from inside the mind to the extra-mental.
There are two different kinds of knowable objects: 1) the
various features of *particular* material things (which are grasped
in sensory knowing); and 2) the *universal* meanings derived
from sense experience (which are known through intellectual
understanding). To see and feel this pen in my hand is a matter of sense perception but to understand that it is a writing
instrument, like many others, is an act of intellection.

Corresponding to these two different levels of knowing
are two different kinds of appetition. One may react affectively to individual things that are sensed or to universals that
are understood. Sense appetition is the response in one's feelings to sense objects; intellectual appetition, willing, is one's
affective response to universal objects of understanding. At
one point Aquinas puts this difference neatly, saying: "in all
cases the appetitive power (*via appetitiva*) is proportioned to
the apprehensive power by which it is moved; the sensitive appetite is for the particular good (*boni particularis*), while the
will (*voluntas*) is for the universal."[3] In Thomistic psychology
one is not said to will an individual object (say this apple) as
a particular thing but one wills it under the guise of some general value (say the promotion of health) that it may be thought
to possess. The affective inclinations typical of sensory appetition (*passiones animae*) are directed toward or away from some
particular good or evil (*aliquod bonum particulare*); whereas the
volitional inclinations proper to the will are directed toward
or away from objects whose rational meaning (*ipsam boni ra-
tionem*) is understood intellectually.[4]

Sense appetition, or passion, is divided by Aquinas into two categories requiring two distinct powers. The difference depends on the kinds of objects that are perceived: some material things are viewed as relatively simple goods or evils, to these the concupiscible appetite is assigned. Other sensible objects present some special difficulty associated with their attainment or avoidance, these are the objects of the irascible appetite. For example, a person who sees a red pepper and desires to eat it is moved in his concupiscible appetite to the act of eating. If he is surprised and angered to find it very hot, this feeling response may move him to spit it out, and this emotion is a movement of the irascible appetite.

Responses on the level of sense appetition are called passions of the soul by Aquinas but our modern word for them is emotions. Etymologically this term is quite suitable, for it suggests an outward motion (ex and motione) in regard to an object of sense cognition. Three positive concupiscent emotions are considered basic by Aquinas: 1) love or liking, a feeling of approval for a perceived particular good; 2) desire, an affective inclination to possess or use such a good; and 3) joy or fruition, a feeling of satisfaction accompanying the attainment of such a good, or of the successful avoidance of an individual evil object. In regard to sense objects perceived as not good (evils) there are three contrasting emotions that are basic: 1) dislike or hate, disapproval of what is seen as not good; 2) aversion, a feeling prompting one to avoid such an evil; and 3) sorrow, an emotion of sadness or frustration in relation to some sensory evil that has not been escaped, or in regard to some sensory good that is too difficult to attain. These six concupiscible emotions are various feeling responses to individual objects perceived as simply good or evil.

Where sense objects are known as associated with some problem or difficulty, either in regard to their attainment or their avoidance, the feelings that are aroused lie on the level of irascibility in the broad sense. Here Aquinas discussed five key passions. Hope is the feeling that one may be able to attain something that is hard to get, or to avoid some threatening evil thing. Despair is the contrasting passion, a feeling that one cannot avoid a threatening evil thing, or that one can never secure a good that is too difficult. Daring or boldness is a feeling that one is able to attack and overcome whatever difficulty is associated with an object of sense perception that one hopes to achieve or avoid. Similarly fear is the recoil emotion felt in connection with an evil perceived as unavoidable. Lastly anger is the feeling of frustration in regard to some evil that has not been avoided because it is beyond one's powers, or a similar feeling connected with failure to secure some desired sense good that is unattainable.[5]

If the foregoing description of eleven chief sensory emotions appears unduly complicated, one might compare it with any article on the emotions in a psychology textbook or an encyclopedia. This area of psychological analysis will be found to be still a great problem. A recent study by Robert C. Solomon on human passions makes a valiant effort to bring some order and light into what he calls, "The Myth and Nature of Human Emotion."[6] In a ninety-page chapter he lists and discusses some forty main passions. The result is informative and well worth reading but obviously much too complex an analysis for those who might wish to use it in legal procedure. On the other hand Aquinas' eleven sensory feelings are basic emotions and may be seen usually to apply to most facets of human affective response. Many other emotions for which we have English names turn out to be but ramifications of these eleven passions.

The human will and its various acts of willing have been understood in a wide variety of ways throughout the history of philosophy and psychology.[7] Thomas Aquinas equated will with intellectual appetite and considered its formal objects to be universal goods or values. With such a meaning one wills items such as peace, health, justice, and so on. Of course Aquinas thought that this intellectual appetite is distinctive of man, as opposed to irrational animals, and he regarded the will as the seat of all man's affective responses to things understood as general goods or evils. So, when a person feels liking or disliking on the sensory level there is usually a parallel movement on the level of willing. Since man is a rational agent, he cannot avoid the responsibility of evaluating and controlling, as far as possible, his emotional impulses by understanding and willing what he judges to be right. This brings us to the heart of the problem of analyzing the experiences that provide the psychological base for moral and legal responsibility. Thomas Aquinas was convinced that rational (that is, intellectual and volitional) control of all emotional responses is advisable but he saw the possibility that extreme cases of passion (such as anger or fear) may not be entirely subject to control by man's reason. Obviously these emergency emotions may get beyond personal control and thus have an important bearing on voluntariness and legal responsibility.

However there is another and very distinctive analysis of willing offered by St. Thomas at the beginning of the Second Part of his *Summa of Theology*.[8] This is a description of intellectual appetition in terms of the means-end relation. In regard to a good viewed as an end, Aquinas thought that *wishing* (*velle*) is a simple act of volitional approval but *intention* (*intendere*) is a more definite act of inclining toward doing something about the end. (Thus most people approve of peace but fewer people form an intention actually to promote peace.) On the other hand, goods regarded as means to an end require intellectual deliberation as to their suitability and a corresponding volitional *consent* (*consensus*) to the appropriate means. Following this consent may come the actual choice (*electio*) of the means to be used. It is at the moment of choice that Aquinas puts the focal point of personal freedom. Choice is a combined activity of the intellect judging and the will committing the person to a definite action or omission.

The final two kinds of will-act in this series are concerned with what Aquinas terms "commanded" actions. These are the overt (usually bodily) acts that only become of ethical importance when they are capable of being controlled and willed by the agent. Thus the act of killing a man is not necessarily voluntary: it may become so, if it comes under the rational command of the acting person. One type of will-act which implements such command is called *use* (*usus*): this is the action whereby one wills to perform (and usually does perform) the external act under consideration. (This helps to clarify, for instance, the meaning of "malice aforethought" in the legal definition of murder.) It is by use that one finally translates thought into commanded activity. Another kind of will-act in this area of execution is called *fruition* (*fruitio*). This consists in the volitional satisfaction that accompanies or follows the commanded act. To take pleasure in doing (or omitting) something marks the climax of volitional approval. And similarly, to regret the performance of a commanded action is to diminish, or in some cases abolish, responsibility for the action.

Now, in the first chapters of the seventh book of the *Nicomachean Ethics*, Aristotle had investigated the problem of what he called *akrasia*, moral weakness or lack of selfcontrol. Since Aristotle did not recognize a faculty of will, his explanation of this personal defect is made in terms of lack of knowledge, weakness of desire (*orexis*), bad habits, or even physical illness. So the notion that there may be a sort of illness in the mind of some persons involved in objectionable activity is not at all new. Thomas Aquinas read Aristotle in Latin and found the word *akrasia* translated as *incontinentia*. The basic meaning of incontinence, in the moral sense, is lack of self-control. Thus we may still speak of a very angry person as "unable to contain himself." Aquinas noted all the factors discussed by Aristotle in explaining this lack of control but he also insisted that the will is central to all human actions. So, as Thomas saw moral failure or deficiency, it consists in the will being inclined toward wrongdoing by the influence of some passion.[9] Whether in Thomistic psychology there is such a thing as "weakness" in the very power of will is debatable. Certainly Aquinas situated the virtues and vices associated with temperate self-control in the concupiscible appetite. But the vice called incontinence seems to indicate a failure of the will to assert control over disturbing concupiscible or irascible passions. So it appears that lack of voluntariness in a moral or legal agent implies some defects in knowledge (either sensory or intellectual) and certain aberrations in appetition (sensory and/or intellectual).

MODIFIERS OF VOLUNTARINESS

The factors that may influence a person in these four areas of consciousness are many, as Aquinas explained them. He recognized that a human person is not merely an immaterial soul but is an animated body. And he thought that the legal or moral agent is the whole person, not just one or the other faculty. So it is the existing individual man who senses and understands, who feels the various emotions aroused by sense objects, and who performs the several acts of willing means and ends. Faculties are not agents but merely different powers through which the whole person acts and undergoes actions initiated by others.

In the field of cognition one may be influenced in deciding to act, and in commanding other activities, by ignorance of facts or of law. Lack of knowledge may diminish or even completely negate voluntariness. Think of a janitor in an office building whose job it is to turn on the electricity for the elevator every morning. One day he flicks the switch and unknowingly electrocutes a repairman working on the circuits in the basement. Unless there was some negligence on the part of the janitor, this would be a case in which ignorance of the repairman's presence actually caused the homicide. The janitor would not be voluntary or responsible for this death. On the other hand, take the example of a worker who has been erroneously informed by a hiring agent that the state in which he is newly employed imposes no state income taxes. The worker finds out later that he was in error about the state law. Provided he had made every reasonable effort to inform himself about the law, his ignorance of this law might render him not voluntary in failing to pay the tax. (Of course he might be held legally responsible, because in many cases the state has no easy way of determining voluntariness.) However, in cases of homicide, courts do attempt to ascertain the prior conscious attitude of the defendant: that is why not every instance of homicide is deemed murder. The point is that morally, and in some instances legally, it is recognized that ignorance of fact or of law is a cognitive defect that may influence voluntariness and responsibility.

Items in the appetitive area that may affect voluntariness are much more difficult to evalutate. We have already seen that the whole matter of "weakness" of will is quite obscure, because introspection reveals little. We might look at the well-known example of St. Augustine who said in his *Confessions* that he wished for several years to reform his way of living but could not bring himself to the point of willing it. He attributed his failure to the influence of sense passions, of course, but insisted that the root of his moral problem was a perversity of will.[10] A quite different but possible instance of failure to will what is known to be the right thing might be found in the case of a young person fully convinced that it would be best to enter a religious congregation but who simply can't take the final step of doing it. Neither lack of knowledge nor sensuality need be involved here. St. Thomas thought that the meaning of "negligence" was indicated by the etymology, *nec eligens*, not choosing. Possibly some cases of reduced voluntariness or non-voluntariness are attributable to volitional failures to use the means recognized as proper to a given end.

However, it is most obvious that disturbances in the emotional life of a person are of major importance in the assessment of voluntariness. Both Thomas Aquinas and contemporary psychologies stress this point. When people speak of mental illness, it is usually some emotional disorder that is indicated. Certainly some instances of strong passion may diminish or even eradicate voluntariness. But Aquinas held that other passions, even strong ones, may increase an agent's voluntariness.

Take the example of a person who has witnessed a crime: he has clearly seen a man shoot a woman on the street. The witness later gets a phone call telling him he will be killed if he testifies to this in court. Much afraid the witness decides not to testify. Here a negative or contra-emotion of fear is the main motivation for omitting a commanded act. The witness is less than completely voluntary in this case, for if he were not in great fear for his life he would have testified.

Or consider the example of a young man who refuses to enter military service because he detests the whole business of killing other people in order to settle disputes between two countries. His motivation may be partly intellectual and volitional but let us say that he also has a violent dislike of firearms. He just can't bring himself to pick up a gun of any kind. This negative emotion can diminish voluntariness, even though that might not be recognized in a court of law.

Positive or pro-emotions usually work the other way: they tend to increase voluntariness. This is a claim that is well understood in some schools of modern psychology. My favorite example is that of a young prince who is ordered by his royal father to marry a princess from another country, for reasons of state. Out of loyalty to father and country, the prince agrees to the marriage. At this point his motivation is intellectual and volitional: he hasn't seen the girl yet. Now he meets her and finds her very attractive. Her beauty arouses very positive concupiscible emotions. He is infatuated and can hardly wait to get married. Obviously this infatuation increases his willingness to proceed with the agreement. The prince would want to marry this girl even if his father objected. Now this is a case in which a strong pro-emotion helps to make the agent more voluntary. Unfortunately the popular notion today is that a person who falls in love, in the romantic sense, is "out of his mind," as it were. This is not the case. Pro-emotions do not diminish responsibility, except in very rare cases. They are not usually instances of mental illness. They are quite natural and normal movements of the sense appetites. It is quite possible, for instance, for a man or woman who is angered at the sight of a mugging to attack the assailant with an umbrella and drive him off. This justifiable anger need not take away one's ability to think and act rationally. Rather such a pro-emotion can be an important factor in moving some people to perform acts that they rationally approve but which they would not ordinarily do.

In contrast consider the example of a motorist who knows that a bridge has been washed out on a country road. He does not warn another person driving toward the bridge, because he dislikes this driver. Here the passion of hatred is at least partly the cause of omitting the warning. If the hated driver is injured, the motorist may be delighted. His feelings of dislike and delight are pro-the-omission, yet the motorist in this case would seem to be voluntary and blameworthy.

Many examples are complicated in the sense that several psychological factors enter into the commanding of an action. Let us reflect on one such case. A woman decides that her terminally ill husband would be better dead. She interrupts the life-support mechanism that is keeping him alive and he dies. Depending on additional circumstances, she could either be not voluntary at all, or partly voluntary. If she really thinks that she is doing the right thing and is so emotionally disturbed that she cannot see any other way out of her problem, she may be in that condition of consciousness in which voluntary deliberation and decision are impossible. On the other hand her feelings of love and despair may only partly impair her ability to reason and will what is good as she sees it. In that event her action would be somewhat voluntary. Defects in her understanding of the technical terms used by physicians and in her sense perception of the condition of her husband might be additional cognitive influences on her degree of voluntariness. This is clearly a very difficult sort of case and few experts would be wise enough to appreciate what was going on in this woman's consciousness. Yet courts are faced, at times, with equally difficult cases.

Still another factor that may modify voluntariness is habit. Often enough, people will say that a malefactor is not responsible for his bad actions because they are the result of bad habits. Thus a boy who grows up in a poor neighborhood and sees most of his peers stealing and taking drugs may be viewed as unlikely to acquire good habits. On the other hand there is a tendency in many of us to think that a child raised in a very proper family under favorable social conditions, and who seems habitually to do the right thing, is not entitled to much credit for his good behavior. Sometimes too, a person will say, "I wish I could stop smoking or drinking or eating excessively but I can't, because I have the habit of so acting."

Now my doctoral dissertation was on Thomas Aquinas' theory of habituation.[11] There are things known today about the physiological aspects of habit formation that Aquinas did not know. However he did develop a remarkable explanation of psychic habits and their influence. Bodily skills, such as swimming, typewriting or piano-playing, are not the sort of habits that are of primary concern in Thomistic psychology. These types of dexterity or automatism are not of great importance in understanding voluntariness. Morally important are the kinds of habits that actually modify one's intellectual, volitional and emotional functioning. Aquinas did not think that the various powers of sense cognition admit of habit formation. That is because the ability to perceive things through the senses is not improved with use, even if the use be well managed. We may train ourselves to use sight or hearing better but that is a matter of rational control; after infancy one's sense perception does not usually get better. Without going into the metaphysics of potency and act (which would be necessary for a thorough study of the Thomistic notion of *habitus*), one might simply say that repeated good use of the intellect, the will, and the sensory appetites enables a person to do things that unpractised people cannot do. Thus a mathematician has an acquired skill or habit of thinking that is simply lacking in the non-mathematician. A habitually just or charitable person has a quality of willing that is an expertness at desiring and doing what is good for others. A temperate person has a quality of self-control in the field of concupiscence which enables one to be moderate without great effort. Similarly a prudent man finds it easy to reason practically and a courageous person finds fortitude a second nature. These are good habits or virtues. They do not lessen the voluntariness of their possessors; on the contrary they increase it.

Contrasting with such good habits are vices. Bad habits are also acquired dispositions of man's higher powers. Unfortunately there are more vices than virtues. On the whole, morally bad habits do not diminish voluntariness or excuse one from responsibility for immoral or illegal activity. Of course there are exceptional instances of people who grow up in social conditions that almost completely determine them to objectionable conduct. But some degree of personal control of thinking, willing and feeling usually remains in such persons. To this extent they are capable of at least partly voluntary action. Indeed this is the basis for rehabilitation programs in prisons.

TERMINOLOGICAL PRECISIONS

One matter becomes evident from the foregoing: it is quite necessary to use terms for psychic experiences in a very precise way. Just as every kind of work tends to develop its own special terminology, so should psychology. But today different schools of philosophy and psychology use diverse terms—and they give quite different meanings to commonly used words. This makes for misunderstanding and lack of real communication. We have noted that such diversity now obtains in the usage of terms associated with willing. But the key term that requires added precision is the word "voluntary" and its modifications. We have seen enough to realize that voluntary cannot simply be equated with the word "willing." When Dickens wrote, "Barkus is willing," he did not mean that he was voluntary.

In point of fact voluntary does not designate one single and invariable mental attitude. It is possible for a person to be

voluntary in different degrees. Between perfect voluntariness
and complete non-voluntariness lies a graded scale of personal
commitment. Consider a person who takes on a new job. He
does so voluntarily: but is he perfectly in favor of it? Possibly
he has been rejected in applying for a better position, or his
working hours are awkward, or the work is rather dangerous,
or his wife doesn't approve of that kind of work. In regard to
most important decisions in life we are partly voluntary and
partly involuntary. It would promote clarity to use the term
"not-voluntary" for the condition that is contradictory to voluntary. Then the term "involuntary" could stand for the condition that is only contrary to voluntariness. In the experience
of the merchant who throws away his goods to avoid ship-
wreck there is a good deal of repugnance to this act, yet he
grudgingly agrees to do it. He is voluntary but not completely
so. We should say that the merchant is somewhat involuntary
in this situation but we could not call him not-voluntary.

The foregoing throws some light on the meaning of
"diminished responsibility" as the term is used in some cases.
Say a person is driving home from a medical or dental appoint-
ment and is somewhat under the influence of a necessary
medication. If an accident occurs due to this condition, it
might be argued that the patient should not have been driving. However there are occasions in which it could not have
been foreseen that the medication would seriously impair the
patient's driving ability. In that event, from a moral point of
view, the patient would not be fully responsible for the bad
result. Nor would it be unreasonable for a court to give consideration to the extenuating features of this sort of case.
Voluntariness may be somewhat decreased in this type of situation by virtue of a temporary physiological impairment.

Another area of ambiguity in the use of terms lies in
speaking of "intention." Derived from the Latin *in* and *tendere*
(to incline towards), this word originally meant to tend toward
a certain end. This is the way that Aquinas employs *intentio*
when writing about moral matters: *intentio primo et principaliter
pertinet ad id quod movet ad finem* (first and foremost intention

applies to whatever moves toward an end).[12] But Webster gives this teleological meaning as secondary to the broader one: "a determination to act in a certain way or to do a certain thing."[13] This, however, is what Thomas speaks of as *consent*, the will-act that follows intellectual deliberation on the appropriate means to secure an end. Thus used, consent signifies a volitional adoption of these means.[14] Consider the example of a seventeenth-century physician who bleeds a patient in order to restore his good health. Here good health would be the end intended but blood-letting would be consented to as a means then considered beneficial. It is confusing to think and speak of both of these volitional acts as intention. Such confusion is sometimes evident in legal discussions of malice.

A moment of attention might also be directed to the expression "mental illness," now being used more and more frequently in connection with the insanity plea. The phrase represents an effort to apply what we know, or think we know, about bodily illness to the quite different sphere of consciousness. But it is amusing to note that much legal debate centers on the problem of pregnancy in labor law. Is the pregnant woman ill by virtue of this condition, or is she simply in a condition that is quite natural for females in any species? If pregnancy is an illness in a worker, then it merits certain special treatment under labor laws (time off and payment of medical expenses). This problem merely illustrates how vague is our notion of, and usage of, the term mental illness. On the surface it may seem a good move to speak of unusual mental conditions as illnesses. Indeed the original meaning of the term "insanity" was unsoundness or illness of mind. But while the words seem familiar in popular usage, the whole idea of mental illness is far from being well understood.

Finally we might note that the proposed new plea, "guilty but insane," is subject to serious criticism from the point of view of Thomistic psychology. The purpose to which this guilty but insane plea is directed seems laudable enough. It is to avoid the situation in which a defendant is found not guilty of a crime, because of insanity, but is committed to an institution until such time as he is found to be sane or not a potential threat to society. In some cases such a verdict results in an early release of a quite dangerous person. But there is something logically odd in the phrase, "guilty but insane." If a defendant is really guilty, then he must be thought to be at least partly voluntary in regard to his action, and so somewhat responsible for it. However, if he is also deemed insane in the usual legal sense, then he is not responsible for the act. Surely it is of no great value to introduce an expression that is fraught with such ambiguity.

FOUR FINAL CONCLUSIONS

By way of conclusion, four points may be made:

I. Much more philosophical thinking on this subject is needed today. We lack even a working terminology to deal with the various analytic factors of consciousness that precede and accompany the decision to perform a responsible act. A 1981 article in the *Journal of Psychiatry and Law* reviews the research literature on the psychological background of this problem and concludes that there is a shocking lack of solid information on this topic.[15]

II. Aquinas' analysis of the factors involved in the voluntary situation is well worth attention today. With the general abandonment of a faculty psychology we lost some of the analytic principles that facilitate a study of voluntariness and ethico-legal responsibility. Yet our courts continue to use some terminology derived from late medieval and early modern Scholastic philosophy.

III. The insanity plea should be retained in our courts, not only for good legal reasons but also because, in spite of some possible miscarriages of justice, there is sound ethical reasoning behind the view that in some cases a human agent is not responsible, or only partly reponsible, for a given act, due to the fact that his voluntariness was diminished or eradicated by a variety of cognitive and emotive defects. For sound philosophical reasons the attempt to substitute a "guilty but insane" plea should not be supported.

IV. Ethicists could well pay more attention to the data and problems that arise in jurisprudence and legal practice. The courts provide a rich source of material for ethical reflection. Perhaps one of the unforeseen results of the Hinckley case may be a growing realization of the need for philosophical studies on the nature of agency, imputability and responsibility for voluntary activity.

Center for Thomistic Studies
University of St. Thomas

NOTES

1. For a brief popular summary of this history see: Irving R. Kaufman, "The Insanity Plea on Trial," *New York Times Magazine* (August 8,1982) pp. 16-20. Judge Kaufman authored the opinion in the Freeman case of 1966.

2. Much of St. Thomas' psychology is condensed in the treatise on the soul, *Summa Theologiae*, I, 75-90 (hereafter *ST*), but it is expanded throughout the Second Part of *ST*. The meaning of "voluntary" (*voluntarium*) is discussed in I-II, 6. Further information on his moral psychology is in Books II and III of the *Commentary on the Sentences*, in the *Disputed Questions De veritate*, 21-26, and *De malo*, 2-6, and in the Commentary on Aristotle's *De anima*, book III.

3. *ST*, I, 64, 2.

4. *ST*, I, 59, 1. A more thorough account of sensory appetition is found later in *ST*, I, 81, and of willing in 82.

5. For a description of the six concupiscible and five irascible passions see: *De veritate*, 26, 4.

6. This is the subtitle of Solomon's book, *The Passions* (Garden City, N.Y.: Doubleday, 1976). See ch. II, pp. 283-373 for his treatment of "The Emotional Register."

7. Vernon J. Bourke, *Will in Western Thought* (New York: Sheed & Ward, 1964) treats eight different meanings of will.

8. On the various acts of willing see: *ST*, I-II, 11-16. A table of these is given in Vernon J. Bourke, *Ethics* (New York: Macmillan, 1966) pp. 59-66.

9. In explaining how the intemperate person is morally worse than one who is incontinent, Thomas says that the intemperate man is so by his own volitional choice but in the case of incontinence, "voluntas inclinatur ad peccandum ex aliqua passione," *ST*, II-II, 156, 3.

10. Augustine, *Confessions*, Bk. II, ch. 1 and 2; Bk. VIII, ch. 5.

11. For a summary of my findings see: "The Role of Habitus in the Thomistic Metaphysics of Potency and Act," in *Essays in Thomism*, ed. R.A. Brennan, O.P. (New York: Sheed & Ward, 1942) pp. 101-109, 370-373.

12. *ST*, I-II, 12, 1.

13. Webster's Collegiate Dictionary (1948) p. 525.

14. *ST*, I-II, 15, 1-4.

15. Richard A. Pasewark, "Insanity Plea: a Review of the Research Literature," *Journal of Psychiatry and Law*, IX, 4, (1981) 357-401.

The Concept of Nature: Avicenna and Aquinas

James A. Weisheipl, O.P.

In this paper, I would like to consider a word that is fundamental not only to all of philosophy, but common to all western languages. That is the word "Nature" and its derivatives "natural," "naturalist," "naturally," "naturalize" and the like. It is so common a term that few even bother to look it up in the dictionary or analyze its precise meaning. We think we know what is meant. Yet on reflection we see that the term is used in all sorts of loose ways. Nature lovers think of the great outdoors; naturalists immediately think of minerals, plants or animals, while philosophers commonly think of some "universe" out-there, a meaning more or less synonymous with that of the Greek word *kosmos*, which means an ordered beauty. The dictionary ordinarily refers to a thing's essential and innate quality or way of acting without explanation or examples. Lawyers today have a great deal to say positively or negatively about what is called "the natural law," without having much to say about what is "natural." All of these uses, and many more, can be traced back to ancient usage, but none of them focus on the precise philosophical meaning from which all other uses of the term are derived.

The ancient Greek philosophers, all of the early Fathers of the Church, and the medieval scholastics were very much concerned with the precise meaning of the term "nature." Christian theologians were particularly concerned about the term because they had to talk about the one nature of God in

65

three divine persons, and about the two natures in Christ. Renaissance humanists often distinguished between Nature with a capital "N," meaning God, and nature with a small "n," meaning the universe created by God. Strangely, even in this context of the humanists, the dynamic character of ancient usage was there only by implication, but never explicated. In the scientific revolution of the 17th century, particularly in England, there was much talk about "the two books"; the book of Nature and the book of Revelation (the Bible). And it was here that the term "nature" took on, what might be called the *static* mold that we assume today. In the mechanistic universe of matter and motion promulgated by Cartesians and Newtonians alike, "nature" was whatever inevitably took place out-there in the objective world of science and mathematical laws of push and pull. The bodies "out there" were thought of as *inert* or moving uniformly with inertial motion—motion and rest being equivalent states—that needed *external force* to alter its state. In this mechanistic universe the term "nature" becomes completely *static*, and the only "laws of nature" that are conceded are deterministic laws of *mechanics* and mathematics. It is hard for us today to avoid thinking in clear and distinct mechanistic terms. But if we cannot get out of that "static mold" we will never begin to understand the dynamic implications of the term "nature," implications which are still there in our every-day speech.

To facilitate a better understanding of the dynamic implications of the older idea of nature, we should say a word about the terms we use every day. As most of our terminology is derived from Latin or Greek, we should begin with them. The Greek word for our term "nature" is one with roots in the distant past; it is *physis*, from which we get our English words "physics," "physical," "physician," and the like. In Greek antiquity, long before Aristotle, the word *physis* had a very precise meaning in a highly technical vocabulary. Technically it meant "a *source* (*arché*, principle) from which movement proceeds to possessing an end (*telos*, goal, purpose, or final cause)." In that definition three aspects are involved: (1) a source "from which," (2) something, such as activity, coming from the source, (3) a goal or quality possessed as a term. These three aspects were very much implied in the Latin term *natura* from which we get our English term "nature." Sometimes the Greek word *physis* and the Latin word *natura* were used in the static sense of the "cosmos" or the "universe," as we sometimes use the term "nature" today. But more often than not, something much more was intended, namely a rich source of dynamic activity and possession of typical qualities or goals. It is in this latter sense that we say, "Let nature take care of it," or "Nature heals," or "It is only natural."

Of course, one does not need to analyze terms philologically or philosophically. But if one wants to appreciate ancient Greek and medieval Latin philosophy, or to appreciate the literature of those ages, one does need to know the meaning of this term and the various ways in which it was understood. In the area of ancient philosophy it is important to appreciate the profoundly different views of Plato and Aristotle regarding *physis*. In the Middle Ages both Avicenna and St. Thomas claimed to be explaining Aristotle's *Physics* and expounding Aristotle's precise definition. Yet Avicenna and Aquinas have radically incompatible views of "nature," much like Plato and Aristotle themselves. Unless one can see precisely how Avicenna and Aquinas differed in their understanding of nature, much of medieval philosophy, literature, and culture will escape us. Or even if we wish only to understand St. Thomas' philosophy, theology, and spirituality better, we will have to appreciate at least the main characteristics of his concept of "nature." Since, however, this older, dynamic meaning of nature is so different from our mechanistic ideas, it will not be easy to grasp. Still, I shall try to explain the philosophical and technical terms as clearly as I can.

In this paper I would like to do two things. First, I would like to explain Aristotle's concept of "nature" in the context of his natural philosophy, for it is here that the notion of "nature" properly belongs. Second, I would like to show how Avicenna and Aquinas differed on three important points in

their understanding of the term. Then I hope to conclude by
showing some of the implications of this contrast for medieval
thought.

I

The best way to approach Aristotle's ideas is through
problems, problems already posed by his predecessors and often
left unresolved by them. If one has no *question*, one cannot
hope to find an answer. Or better, we may have a "fact," but
no question to which the "fact" could be an answer. One
reason, I think, why Aristotle's writings are so difficult is that
we often skip the "problem" before his eyes. It is like reading a "response" in St. Thomas' *Summa* and skipping the
"Videtur quod non" and the "Sed contra," or like memoriz-
ing answers in the Catechism without noticing the questions.
Not only Aristotle, but Plato too, must be seen in terms of the
problem posed by his predecessors. Briefly, Aristotle tried to
restore to dignity the ancient, pre-Socratic quest for some rational explanation of the way things are or seem to be in the
physical world in which we live. He tried, in fact, to restore
natural philosophy as a truly "scientific" quest, in the face of
Plato's opinion that all such investigations are futile, ending,
as they must, in *opinion*, or *doxa*, merely a "likely story."

The history of ancient Greek philosophy, as I see it, can
be seen as three stages of a quest. First, the pre-Socratics who
really did try to discover the causes of things, causes that
would answer the question "Why?" As far as natural philosophy is concerned, they can be called *physiologoi* in the technical sense, meaning philosophers who sought the "nature"
(*physis*) of things around us, i.e., the "nature" or stuff of which
we and the universe are made. We are told that Socrates, too,
as a young man, was a *physiologos* searching for the causes of
which the universe is made. But, seeing the endless difficulties
and the variety of answers given by others, he gave up the
search for "natures" (*physis*) and turned to "soul" (*psyche*), a

much more important quest. With Socrates comes Plato, who claimed that real causal (or "scientific") explanations can be given only in mathematics, particularly in geometry. This is the only area of human knowledge that Plato calls "epistemic" or "scientific." Higher than this area, for Plato, is *dialectics*, or what would later come to be called "First Philosophy" or Meta-physics. That is to say, Plato abandoned the philosophical quest for "natures" *out of which* the sensible world is made and turned his attention to "Soul" (*psyche*) and the permanent things of Mind (*nous*). With Aristotle one reaches a third stage of Greek philosophy, which is basically an attempt to reinstate the quest for "natures" as something worthy of study and certain in its own limited right. Without abandoning the study of *psyche*, Aristotle thought that *physis* too should be studied. In fact, for Aristotle, the only way to establish the existence of "soul," "mind" or any immaterial substance is through physics. In any case, this is the way I see the development of science and the origin of philosophy among the ancient Greeks; both St. Thomas and St. Albert also give this threefold classification of the history of philosophy, although they use different names.

But let us return to the pre-Socratic *physiologoi* who looked for the principles and causes out of which this tangible universe is made. It turns out that many of the pre-Socratic philosophers were materialists, admitting either one or many first principles. At least that is the way Albert and Thomas saw them, following Aristotle. The main point is that those *physiologoi* who posited matter as the *physis* of all things thought of "nature" as the "source" or "principle" from which all reality comes. *Physis* for them was not a "thing" but a principle (*arché*) out of which all things are made, past, present and future. Whether this "nature" was one element or many elements was secondary; the point is that the only kind of *physis* admitted by these *physiologoi* was material. That is, in the terms of Aristotle, they admitted only a material cause, but an *active* material cause to account for the *genesis* or production of things. A different group of philosophers, generally called

Pythagoreans, thought that the *physis* of all things was "number," which begot figure and the form of things. While Aristotle disagreed with the Pythagoreans, he thought of them as discussing the "formal" cause of things rather than the matter. Even here, however, Aristotle would insist that there is something more specific than number as the "form" of each and every type of material thing. But if "form," too, accounts for the way a thing behaves, it, too, should be called a "nature" (*physis*) even more properly than matter.

One entire book of Aristotle's *Metaphysics*[1] is a philosophical lexicon in which he traces the origin and development of technical words. One such word is *physis*, which he says originally meant the begetting of living things, i.e., the actual *process* of begetting and growing. By the time of Aristotle the word no longer had this restricted meaning of begetting, but it seems that the Latin word *natura* originally meant the process of giving birth, *naturans*, from which we get our word "nativity" for "birth," "native," and "naturalize." But very soon, Aristotle says, the term was transferred to the origin or source of this begetting, an active source *from which* things are begotten. Therefore when the pre-Socratics sought the "nature" of things in "water," "air," "infinite" or the like, they were looking for an *active source* of all things. But the "matter" which was posited, for Aristotle, is *not active*; in fact, it needs to be *acted upon*. Therefore Aristotle distinguished, on the one hand, an active source of a thing already existing—he called this the "form" or "whatness" of a thing—and, on the other hand, the active source responsible for a thing *coming into being*—this he called the "agent" cause or "effective" (efficient) cause, thus conceiving the "form begotten" as the end product (*telos*) of generation.

In all of this you can see the source of Aristotle's four causes: the agent producing, the product produced (formal and final), matter *from which* the product is produced. But never does Aristotle or anyone else call the efficient or final cause "nature" (*physis*). It is only the material and formal causes. Matter, for Aristotle, can rightly be called "nature" as the passive recipient, the source *out of which* things are made. On this score the ancient *physiologoi* were right in seeing matter as one kind of "nature." But, for Aristotle, a far greater reality is the *physis* (or "nature") that makes a thing to be *what* it is and to act the *way* it does. This "nature" Aristotle called "form," an active principle of being and acting. That is, "form," as the nature of a thing, is the source responsible for the thing having the characteristics it does have and acting the way we see it act, consistently.

Thus Aristotle defines "nature" as the "principle and cause of activity and rest in those things in which it exists properly (*per se*) and not incidentally (*per accidens*)." Aristotle gives this definition at least thirteen times in whole or in part throughout his writings. Therefore it is important to understand what he means by "nature" and the philosophy of "nature." The first point is that for him nature is an efficient cause only (i) of self-motion in animals and (ii) of certain effects in other things, like fire burning wood; of all other things, nature is only a "principle"—both passive as in matter and active as in form—and not a cause strictly so called. It differs from "chance" in being usual, normal and *per se*; and from "art" (*techne*) in being independent of human interference or "mind." Thus "natural" things for Aristotle would be anything usually and normally produced by "nature," such as animals, trees, man, the elements, and their parts.

The "nature" that makes a thing to be *what* it is Aristotle called substantial form, and the whole composite, *ousia* or substance. It was for him a real, objective principle of specific characteristics and activities, and an efficient cause of (i) its own motion (in the case of animate things) and (ii) of certain effects in others, as fire heating water or burning wood. The Latin scholastics of the Middle Ages talked about "Nature" in the widest possible sense as "form" or *natura secundum principium activum seu formale*, and as "matter" or *natura secundum principium passivum, receptivum seu materiale*. In the former sense it would extend to any action or reaction even of the elements, while in the latter sense it would include any passivity an element would have, even, in a certain sense, receptivity for human use, as in art and mechanics.

Perhaps the main point to keep in mind is that for Aristotle all bodies that actually exist have some kind of "nature," i.e. active and passive abilities, not only to *be* what they are, but also to *act* the way they do and to *be affected* in limited ways. For him no *corpus* is entirely devoid of active and passive characteristics. Descartes and Newton, on the other hand, thought of bodies as mere extension and as inert, a *corpus nudum*. Such a conception, for Aristotle, would be true only of a mathematical body, a *corpus mathematicum* abstracted from nature. Natural philosophy, for Aristotle, was the study of everything that exists in the physical world, and all things happened to have different "natures" with different propensities and structures, ranging from inanimate elements to plants, animals, and man. This was the vast area envisaged by all Aristotelians as the philosophy of nature, vastly different from mathematics, metaphysics, or moral philosophy, but the basis of all other knowledge, even art and technology.

II

Avicenna, the Persian Muslim of the 11th century, considered himself to be an Aristotelian in the sense that Aristotle's philosophy was the main source of his own thought. But Avicenna was also influenced by Platonic thought and the Koran, the sacred book of the Muslims. Many of Avicenna's writings came into the Latin West through Spain in the second half of the 12th century; at the same time Aristotle's own works were being translated from Arabic in Spain, and from Greek in Italy. It was all part of the "new learning" that molded Latin Scholasticism in its views about God, man and nature. Avicenna's view of "nature" was distinctive of his personal philosophy. Its impact on Arabic thought and on Christians in the Latin West was enormous. No one can begin to understand the writings of St. Albert, St. Thomas, Henry of Ghent, or Duns Scotus without some understanding of Avicenna's natural philosophy, particularly his understanding of "nature" and of Aristotle's definition.

In this paper I would like to consider three elements in Avicenna's understanding of Aristotle's definition of "nature": (1) the kind of causality involved in inanimate natural motions, such as the falling of heavy bodies and the rising of light bodies; (2) the real cause of all natural substantial changes, such as water changing to air, the generation of animals, and the burning of wood; (3) the place of "chance" in the world of nature, and even free will in the case of man. All these elements can be found in Avicenna's paraphrase of Aristotle's *Physics* called *Sufficientia* in the Latin translation from Arabic by Dominic Gundissalinus in the 1150s. These three elements were also summarized by Algazel in his *Macâcid el-falâcifa*, also translated by Gundissalinus in the 1160s, and usually referred to as Algazel's *Metaphysics*.

The first and foremost element we wish to consider has to do with the precise meaning of "nature" as an active or "formal" principle of motion and rest in all bodies, animate or inanimate, the typical case being the falling of heavy bodies and the rising of light. Throughout *Sufficientia* Bk I, cc.5-9, Avicenna equates *natura* with a kind of force (*vis* or *virtus*) found differently in different bodies, such as "forces" in a celestial body due to an *anima angelica*, forces in animals due to an *anima sensibilis*, in plants due to an *anima vegetalis*, and in inanimate bodies all movement and forces due to *natura* properly so called. This last type of "nature," i.e., in inanimate bodies, Avicenna defines as "the source of its movements and its actions." What is unique in Avicenna's view is that "nature" as a source in all these bodies (celestial, animate, plant, and inanimate) is always called an "efficient cause" of motion. In other words, even after a particular nature is brought into existence by a generator, which is an external efficient cause, "nature" itself is the *internal efficient cause* of all that it does, like falling down or rising in the case of light bodies. Thus the "nature" of a heavy body is the efficient cause of its downward movement, just as the "nature" of a plant is the efficient cause of its sprouting of roots, stalk, buds

and seeds. Avicenna groups inanimate bodies and plants together in that their "natures" do not cause self-motion in the
strictest sense of *ex seipso* since they are devoid of knowledge.
But animals, men, and angels are grouped together in that the
"natures" in these creatures are *aware* of some goal (or final
cause) toward which they move themselves *ex seipsis*.

Avicenna, in other words, conceives "nature" even in
inanimate bodies as a "mover," a *motor coniunctus*, a conjoined efficient cause accompanying the body it moves. On
this score, all motion is a kind of self-motion, effectively produced by a "nature" which accompanies the body it moves as
a *motor coniunctus*. Only from this point of view can one understand why Henry of Ghent, Duns Scotus and many others
rejected St. Thomas' first proof for the existence of God: natural bodies do not need *to be moved* by another (*ab alio*), for
they move themselves as spirits do.

The problem St. Thomas saw in Avicenna's interpretation was a serious one. If "nature" is an efficient cause, a
mover, and a vital force (*vis viva*) within the inanimate bodies,
how does it differ from the self-mover in animals? If a heavy
body is said to move itself down when released, how does this
motion differ from a bird swooping down to the worm on the
ground? How is the man walking down the stairs different from
a man falling down the stairs? Avicenna (and Duns Scotus
after him) says that animals, men, and angels *know* where they
are going, whereas stones do not. But is there no difference in
the movement itself? Does not the kind of motion a falling
stone has differ from the self-movement of an animal?

Commenting on Aristotle's definition in the *Physics* II,
c.1, St. Thomas takes great pains to distinguish a *principium*
from a *causa*, an active principle from a producing cause.
While every cause is a principle for Thomas, not every principle is a cause, least of all an efficient cause. In itself, a principle is a generic term, meaning the *beginning*, like the point
beginning the line, the dawn beginning the day, the first line
beginning the book, etc. It is the "source" of what comes from
it, namely the *principiatum*, and it can be grasped only in terms
of what comes from it. That is, a "principle" can be understood as a *source* only in reference to the *principiatum* coming
from it. "The generic term principium is placed in the defini-

tion of 'nature,'" Thomas says, "not as something absolute (*aliquid absolutum*), but as a relative term (*quid relativum*) related to what comes from it as a source." Thus Thomas rejects any attempt of later authors to correct Aristotle's definition by calling it "a force imbedded in things" (*vis insita rebus*) or something of that sort (Lect. 1, n.5).[3]

St. Thomas does indeed admit that sometimes "nature" is an efficient cause of certain limited activities, as when an animal moves itself through its parts (*per partes*), and when one nature affects another, like fire burning wood or changing water into air. In the first case (of Fido running), an animal is truly the efficient cause of its own movement, namely walking, running, crawling, flying, swimming and the like, where its exercise of causality is in part moving part. Such self-movement is possible only in living organisms having organs. In the second case (of fire burning wood), at least for Thomas, the "nature" of one body can be a true efficient cause of an effect in another body in some sense distinct from itself; this will be considered in a moment. The point at issue here is that inanimate "nature" as a mere formal, active principle cannot be an efficient cause of its own downward or upward movement, no more than a tulip bulb can be said to move itself to grow. On this point St. Thomas is very clear when he says:

> Just as other accidents follow upon the substantial form, so does being in place, and consequently motion toward that place; not however in such a way that the natural form is the mover (*motor*), but the mover is the generator which begot such a form upon which that motion subsequently follows.

This means that when a gentleman falls down the stairs, he is not to blame, but his corporeity is. Likewise the gentleman is not the efficient cause of his blue eyes, his blond hair or his height. These are all works of nature, spontaneous, automatic and necessarily stemming from his make-up—his genes, if you like.

Nature as a formal principle, therefore, can be only a "source" (*arché, principium*) and not a mover, or efficient cause of what comes "naturally" and spontaneously. This must be the case first, because otherwise there would be no way to

distinguish animate from inanimate movement: a man's falling down the stairs and walking down, the rising of fire and
the upward flight of birds. Clearly there is an important difference between my walking down the stairs and my falling
down, between my learning algebra and my having blue eyes.
Second, the movement of all animals involves one part moving another part. But in homogeneous bodies, such as the
elements, the whole quantity is infinitely divisible, and as
Aristotle demonstrated in Book VI of the *Physics*, in a con-
tinuum that is infinitely divisible there can be no "first" part
at all. St. Thomas calls this a *propter quid* demonstration of
why an inanimate body cannot move itself, but must be moved
by another (*In VII Phys.*, lect. 1, n.6). In other words, once
a nature comes into existence by some efficient cause, that
nature does everything it is supposed to do spontaneously, immediately (*statim*), automatically (*in promptu*), and necessarily
(*ex necessitate*), provided there is no obstacle. Some of these actions take time to come about, like growing, and some can
take place many times, like falling down. The *per se* efficient
cause of all these motions can be none other than the original
generator. If, however, there should be an obstacle, the one
who removes this obstacle (*removens prohibens*) can be credited
only *per accidens* and improperly as the "cause" of natural motion, since removal merely permits nature to take its course.

   Incidentally, Avicenna's un-Aristotelian notion of "nature" as an efficient cause of all motions, notably gravitational
motion, is even now working havoc among historians of medieval science, particularly as this notion was seconded and reenforced by Averroes in his influential commentaries on Aristotle. Because of their misinterpretation of Aristotle, the supposed need for a *motor coniunctus* for all motion has been
projected onto Aristotle's so-called dynamics. Some of the
scholastics did, indeed, understand Aristotle's axiom "Everything that is moved is moved by another" to mean that an
efficient cause conjoined to the body is required for all things
in motion. Because of this misunderstanding, Duns Scotus and
Francisco Suarez rejected Aristotle's axiom as a means of proving the existence of God. Avicenna's misinterpretation of
Aristotle, of course, was rejected by St. Thomas throughout
his writings.

The second element to be considered in Avicenna's concept of "nature" has to do with substantial changes we see occurring in nature, as when air is generated from water. The pre-Socratic *physiologoi* always had a problem regarding the possibility of real substantial change: How can one substance cease to be and another come into being? It is the problem of *genesis* (*fieri*), the problem of coming-to-be and passing-away. It is a question of how can a radically new substance come to be? Either the form always existed, in which case it does not come into being: *quod est, non fit*. Or it never existed, in which case it cannot come into being: *ex nihilo, nihil fit*. Aristotle solved this ancient dilemma by distinguishing between "being" *in act* and "being" *in potency*; the new form can be said "to exist" only in potency before it is actually realized. If the new substance were *not able* to be, then no new substance could come to be; but this potency exists in the old substance. What is needed is simply an efficient cause capable of actualizing the potentiality of that matter.

Avicenna faced this same problem in his *Sufficientia* and in his *Metaphysics*, but he never grasped Aristotle's solution embedded in the concept of the *pure potentiality* of first matter (the *materia prima* of the scholastics). For Avicenna, natural agents, i.e., natures existing in material bodies, can only dispose the accidents of matter to such a point that it is immediately receptive to receiving a new substantial form. But whence comes this new form? Avicenna could see no way out but to postulate a separated intelligence, called a *dator formarum*, a giver of forms, or *intellectus agens* separated from all human intellects. This angelic intellect for Avicenna was the tenth in emanation from God, the First Cause of all. The function of this *dator formarum* was twofold: to implant new substantial forms in matter properly disposed by nature, and to instill new knowledge, i.e., intelligible forms in the human mind properly disposed by a good teacher. In both cases it is forms that are implanted in matter disposed by nature: intelligible forms in learning and substantial forms in generation. Of course, there is no such thing as a *dator formarum* in the whole of Aristotle's doctrine. It was invented by Avicenna to explain two difficult problems: substantial changes in nature and new ideas in learning.

Incidentally, Latin scholastics who had similar difficulty in explaining substantial changes and new ideas identified this tenth intelligence in Avicenna with the one God of Christianity. God, then, was not only the "true light which enlightens every man coming into this world,"[4] but also the true efficient cause of all substantial forms, including the human soul. The irony of Avicenna's solution is that he made nature an efficient cause of natural motions produced in the body, but he refused to make "nature" the efficient cause of forms produced in other bodies. For this reason Avicenna invented two kinds of efficient causes: a moving cause or cause of motion (*causa movens* or *movendi*), proper to sensible nature, and an agent cause or cause of being (*causa agens* or *essendi*) proper only to spiritual beings, intelligences. For Aristotle and for St. Thomas, "nature" is the efficient cause "of being" in every production of substantial change, for only substances properly exist and have *esse*.

For St. Thomas there is no need for a *dator formarum* or separated *intellectus agens* to explain human learning or substantial changes in nature. Both are simply the work of "nature." As for human understanding, St. Thomas says that human "nature" in each individual is sufficiently endowed by nature with all the faculties needed for natural knowledge. These faculties of the human soul (*potentiae animae*) include not only the power to see, hear, feel and the like, but also spiritual faculties of intellect, both active and passive, and the will. These faculties or powers come immediately and necessarily from "human nature" as from a formal principle. All that is required once the soul is infused is time and the normal course of development for a mature human being. As for substantial change in the world, Thomas saw no reason why one element, say fire, could not only heat water (an accidental change), but also change water into air (a substantial change). Both Aristotle and Thomas saw all of this as belonging to the terrestrial world of "nature." But both realized the importance of the sun and God as universal or "equivocal" causes of nature and natural processes.

The third and last point of difference between Avicenna and Thomas as they interpreted Aristotle's concept of nature has to do with chance and free will in the universe. As

Avicenna saw it, each nature is pre-determined to act in one specific way; acorns always grow into oak trees. Nature as a principle of motion and rest in each and every body is ordained to a uniquely characteristic end: "nature acts for an end," which is unique for each species. But Avicenna thought that each activity in the concrete had to be regulated by the heavens, just as the more important events of learning and changing were regulated by the least angelic intelligence called *dator formarum*. Thus astrology became for Avicenna, not only a pastime and hobby, but a metaphysics of current and future events regulated by the stars. In effect this eliminated all chance events in nature and all free will in man. He explicitly states that "one and the same thing can be seen from one point to be necessary and frequent, but from another point of view to be free (*utrumlibet*) and occasional; but when all things are perfectly considered, all would agree that it happens of necessity."[5] It is hard to know whether Avicenna's determinism stemmed more from a misunderstood Aristotle or from Koranic fatalism. In either case, "freedom" and "chance," for Avicenna, are mere words that philosophers sometimes use and talk about, as does Aristotle.

For St. Thomas, on the other hand, as for all Christians, freedom is an essential constituent of the human will. Man's actions are in a different category altogether from chance events. This conviction was the one philosophic truth that the Church emphasized time and time again in the thirteenth century. Man's actions are not predetermined by the stars; man is indeed responsible for what he does. But there were not a few in the Middle Ages, who, while exempting the human will, thought everything else was determined by the stars. This view was reenforced by Avicenna's concept of nature and by the astrology of Albumazar.

In Aristotle's world, the concept of "nature" absolutely requires "chance" to account for the unintended and irrational in nature. Nature by definition is a specific *principle* toward a specific *goal* and a characteristic, specific *way* of attaining it. But chance events are always concrete and particular; they are the coincidence of two or more agencies, each one concretely determined toward its own end. "Chance," for Aristotle, is the unintended *encounter* of one cause with another. It is "chance" precisely because it cannot be intended by that nature; if it were, it would be happening all the time, and hence "natural." The natural is exactly what is "intended" by a given nature, and what is "intended" is what usually happens for the most part (*ut in pluribus*). The "good" toward which nature tends and usually attains with its own resources is precisely what we mean by the "final cause" of that nature. There cannot be a "final cause" unless it is a positive "good" for that nature. But there are many occurrences that are not good, sometimes not even in the long run. It is these events that must be termed "chance." If it is a happy event, we call it "good luck" or "fortune"; if it is bad, we call it "bad luck" or "misfortune." In either event, the encounter itself is the one thing that "nature" cannot intend, for then it would be happening all the time. The event may not be *contra naturam*, but it is always *praeter intentionem naturae*. A universe without chance may be a Stoic or Moslem universe or possibly the perfect mechanism of a watchmaker. It certainly is not the universe as Artistotle saw it.

The contrast between Avicenna and Aquinas in the Middle Ages is basically the opposition between Plato and Aristotle in antiquity. Avicenna put too big a gap between material natures run by the stars and the mind of man run by separated intelligences. Within man, he saw too big a gap between the mind of man and his body, a dualism that is not all that different from that of Descartes in the seventeenth century and that of many religions today. From this springs a strange kind of spirituality, one that would flee from the world, from the body as from evil, and retreat into one's self, a retreat that might very well be talking to the spirits. That is, for Avicenna, the mind of man belongs to the angels and his personal conversation may very well be with God, but it is extremely private, since one man's conversation excludes all other minds tied to bodies. St. Thomas, following Aristotle and his Christian principles, saw man himself as part of nature, and his own natural personality as made up of body and soul. In this view, the way to God is *through* nature, for it was this "nature" that God created, and it was this "nature" that Christ redeemed.

A Platonic or idealist flight from nature is, in Thomas' view unrealistic, to say the least; no man can escape from nature, for he himself has a nature and he belongs to the world of nature. Man's happiness therefore is to go through nature to God and thereby sanctify nature and the things of nature, for it is the same God who made nature and sanctified it by his blood.

Pontifical Institute of Mediaeval Studies
Toronto

NOTES

1. Book Delta.
2. Avicenna, *Sufficientia* in *Opera Philosophica* (Venice, 1508), folia 13-36.
3. *Commentaria In Octo Libros Physicorum Aristotelis* in Sancti Thomae Aquinatis Doctoris Angelici *Opera Omnia* Iussu Impensaque Leonis XIII. P.M., t.2 (Rome, 1884).
4. John 1,9.
5. *Sufficientia*, I, c.13,fol. 21 ra.

The Descent of Man
According to Thomas Aquinas

Victor B. Brezik, C.S.B.

In 1871 Charles Robert Darwin published *The Descent of Man. Descent* primarily signifies a coming down from something above. It also has the meaning of lineage. What Darwin meant was lineage and more precisely, the ascent of man, a coming up of man from below by a process of evolution; man's ascent or rise from an animal of the anthropoid group.

Today this view of man is taken for granted. It is widely assumed that man has his total roots, not just his corporeal roots, in matter and that human consciousness is an epiphenomenon entirely dependent on matter.[1] As to his nature man is explainable in terms of physiological and biological laws; as to his behavior he is explainable in terms of psychological laws drawn from animal psychology. There can be no true freedom in man because there is nothing in man that transcends matter and the determinism of matter. As such man can be manipulated and controlled by selected stimuli to perform in an acceptable manner.

These assumptions are the consequences of a conception of man based upon the supposition of his completely animal origin. What arises from the animal is a new species called *man*, a superior species, but still in all respects only animal.

Among scientists and even for the man on the street this anthropological teaching has become almost gospel. It underlies as a silent supposition the investigations carried on under the name of the behavioral sciences and the social sciences as

well. Scarcely anyone questions this view today. But a serious
question is whether there is not some need to question it. For
there can be not only concern about where this view has
brought us in our practical dealings with man; one can even
anxiously wonder where such a trend will end.

The original shock of Darwin's proposal of man's animal
origin has by this time quite thoroughly worn away. Despite
the controversy raised by the proponents of scientific crea-
tionism, some version of human evolution is generally accepted with an air of resignation and perhaps a shrug of the
shoulder. It would in fact be dogmatic at this stage of biological evidence to exclude evolution from speculations about
man's origin. An honest search for truth demands that this
problem remain open to thorough scientific and philosophical
exploration. Yet the acceptance of animal ancestry as a *total*
philosophy of man is far more than an evolution in man's idea
of man. By comparison certainly with the classical Greek and
Christian anthropologies, it is a veritable revolution whose
consequences are not yet fully realized.

Our society and our culture, to some extent at least, still
operate on the assumption that man is political in his nature,
moral in his behavior, religious in his aspirations, and teach-
able in his improvement of self. None of these qualities, however, are strictly animal qualities. They are indicative of a
transcendent principle which surpasses not only what is generic to the animal but goes beyond the highest attainments of
every species of animal other than man. These qualities postulate intellect, will and freedom, all of which are unexplainable
by the mere dimension of matter. No animal as such indisput-
ably manifests in its behavior a capacity for cognition of universal objects, a pursuit of the good itself, deliberate choices
or reflexivity.[2] Only an intellectual nature holds such a capacity which evidently is rooted not in matter but in spirit. This
fact radically changes the concept of man. At the same time,
it puts into question, not the possibility of evolution in the
formation of man's body, but the evolutionistic explanation of
the total nature of man.

The purpose of this paper is not to investigate whether evolution in fact has a part in the explanation of man, nor even whether a doctrine of development suitably fits into a Thomist anthropology.[3] These questions need further study. My purpose is rather to see why evolution considered as a total accounting of human origin, resulting in a materialist concept of man, is incompatible with the Christian tradition represented especially by the anthropology of Thomas Aquinas. The paper will have four main divisions. First, by means of a cursory glance at the views of his predecessors, I shall try to bring into focus the precise problem of man that confronted St. Thomas in the thirteenth century. Secondly, I shall treat of the human soul considered as both form of the body and a subsistent reality. Thirdly, the origin of man and of the human soul in the teaching of St. Thomas will be examined. The conclusion of the paper will follow as the fourth part.

I. THE PROBLEM OF MAN CONFRONTING ST. THOMAS

Man as Seen by St. Thomas' Predecessors

As philosophical speculation subsequent to the materialist viewpoint of the early Greek naturalists progressed, a recognition of the radical distinction between sense and intellect and the immaterial nature of intellectual knowledge is evident in thinkers like Plato and Aristotle and simultaneously with them new philosophical perspectives on human nature occurred. These perspectives determined the anthropological outlook for centuries to come.

If one thing can be said in a general way about the Greek concept of man bequeathed to the western world, it is the conviction that there is something in man that emerges above matter. Man is endowed with reason which differentiates him specifically from all other animals and furthermore reason itself is in some way separate or at least separable from matter.

Even Aristotle, for whom man is essentially a composite of body and soul, hesitated to identify intellect and intellectual activity with matter. For Plato, there was no question at all about the spiritual nature of man. Having identified man with the soul, the body could not be an essential part of man. For this reason, the separation of the soul from the body at death was considered purely as a desirable release of the soul from its bodily prison.

The advent of Christianity brought new dimensions to the concept of man but these were the religious dimensions of man fallen and wounded by original sin and redeemed and healed by the saving grace of Christ. Man's supernatural destiny was now revealed together with the new life in Christ which commences with baptism. There was also acceptance of the revealed doctrine of man's creation in the image of God. *Genesis* had affirmed the composite nature of man in terms of the slime of the earth and the breath of life. Christ's teaching on the resurrection of the body re-emphasized this dual nature of man without detracting from the importance of spirit over the body.

So emphatic indeed was the primacy of the spiritual principle in the Christian concept of man that when St. Augustine in the fourth and fifth centuries came to treat of man he adopted the Platonic concept and, inconsistently with his own Christian convictions, defined man as a rational soul using an earthly and mortal body.[4]

Not until the thirteenth century—when St. Thomas Aquinas was faced with the conflicting currents of Augustinian Christianized Platonism and the Neo-platonized Aristotelianism of the medieval Arabian thinkers — was a consistent philosophical concept of man in harmony with Christian revelation carefully and satisfactorily worked out.

The Central Problem Facing St. Thomas

There were two principal and essential aspects of man that needed to be philosophically defined in order to resolve the tensions in the conflicting currents of medieval thought arising mainly from the deficiencies in the Platonic and the Aristotelian doctrines on man. By identifying man with the soul, Plato was able to argue for the soul's existential independence of the body and its survival after death. What was lacking here was a satisfactory explanation of the soul's union with the body. On the other hand, the accidental union of soul and body in Plato's teaching was corrected in the teaching of Aristotle which explained the substantial unity of man in terms of his concept of the soul as the substantial form of the body. The weakness in Aristotle's explanation is the failure expressly to safeguard the immortality of the soul, for according to his teaching, when a substantial change occurs, the form is simply reduced to the potentiality of matter. In these terms, the human soul, as the form of the body, would not actually survive any separation from the body at the time of death.[5]

Aside from connected questions concerning the correct interpretation of Aristotle's doctrine on the intellect which Arabian thinkers tended to regard as separate from individual human beings, the main problems about man's nature which faced St. Thomas were fairly well defined. The central question was how to reconcile a doctrine of the soul's immortality with a doctrine of the substantial unity of man as a composite of body and soul.

An interesting as well as revealing approach to the question of man is St. Thomas' treatment of the question in Book Two of his *Summa contra gentiles*. Chapter forty-six of Book Two affirms on metaphysical grounds that the perfection of the universe required the existence of some intellectual creatures. Subsequent chapters deal with various aspects of intellectual substances. Finally, after a rather full description of such intellectual substances, i. e. angelic natures, St. Thomas in chapter fifty-six rather abruptly and surprisingly asks in what way an intellectual substance can be united to the body. This chapter fifty-six marks the beginning of his treatise in the *Summa contra gentiles* of the human soul and the nature of man.

The point that strikes one most forcefully in this approach is its apparent affinity with the Platonic concept of
man. There is no question but that St. Thomas is initiating
his treatment of man within the context of his treatment of
intellectual substances. Does this mean that in his eyes man
is a certain kind of intellectual substance, or at least that the
human soul itself is an intellectual substance? If this is the
case, what have we here but another attestation of the Platonic view of man? But in such a case, what is to be done
about the composite nature of man?

II. THE HUMAN SOUL AS BOTH FORM
AND SUBSISTENT

Can the Soul Be Both Form and a Particular Thing?

In all his writings, there is perhaps no instance where St.
Thomas comes to fuller grips with the central problem of man
than in the first article of his *Quaestio de anima*. This article
asks whether the soul can be both a form and a particular
thing (*hoc aliquid*). What St. Thomas understands by a particular thing is "an individual in the genus of substance" which
he identifies with Aristotle's *first substance*. To be a particular
thing implies the possession of two characteristics: first, subsistence; secondly, completeness as to species. In other words,
a particular thing must have the capacity to exist as a distinct
entity with its own existence rather than with an existence in
some other entity as in a subject. And furthermore, it must be
a substance which possesses completely the nature of a species.

Do these two characteristics of a particular thing belong
to the human soul? They certainly do not characterize the
human soul if, like Empedocles, the soul be regarded as a harmony or blending of elemental principles, or if, according to
the view ascribed to Galen, the soul be taken as a combination (*complexio*) of the elements. In either case, the soul would
only be a form similar to other material forms, none of which

can constitute a particular thing, since a material form cannot exist of itself apart from matter.

Views of the soul such as those proposed by Empedocles and Galen, because of their gross materiality, do not even befit the vegetative or the sensitive soul, much less the rational soul of man. This is quite evident with the sensitive soul whose sense operations receive the sensible likenesses of things sensed without the matter of the things sensed. It is more evident still with the rational soul which in its cognitive operation not only receives forms without their matter but beyond this receives them also without the individuating conditions of matter. This happens because the proper mode of knowing for the rational soul is to abstract and abstraction results directly in a knowledge of the universal, not of the individual.

St. Thomas goes on to confirm the argument for the rational soul with evidence which has profound significance respecting the nature of the human soul. In the first place, owing to its transcendence over matter in its operation, the rational soul, at least in its highest activity, intellection, cannot function in conjunction with any bodily organ as it does in the case of the senses. Not only, he says, does the rational soul "receive intelligible species without matter and material conditions, but it is also quite impossible for it, in performing its proper operation, to have anything in common with a bodily organ, as though something corporeal might be an organ of understanding, in the same manner as the eye is the organ of sight."[6]

Something of utmost importance for discerning the nature of the human soul necessarily follows from this. In the words of St. Thomas himself, "thus the intellective soul, inasmuch as it performs its proper operation without communicating in any way with the body, must act of itself."[7] This means that the intellectual operation of the human soul is intrinsically an immaterial operation.

And there is a still more significant consequence. It is that the human soul must be capable of existing in itself in-

dependently of the body. The principle upon which this conclusion is based is the rather evident proposition that a thing
acts or operates so far as it is actual — *quia unumquodque agit
secundum quod est actu*. In this particular case, if the rational
soul is capable of acting independently of matter, it must be
capable of existing independently of matter. The actuality of
operation is proportioned to the deeper actuality of existence.
St. Thomas declares: "Because a thing acts so far as it is actual, the intellective soul must have a complete act of existing
in itself, depending in no way on the body."

Why is this independence from the body necessary? It is
necessary on the same principle taken in reverse. Just as a form
which acts independently of matter must exist independently
of matter, so also a form which depends on matter or on a subject for its existence cannot operate independently of matter.
As St. Thomas says: "Forms whose act of existing depends on
matter or on a subject do not operate of themselves. Heat, for
instance, does not act; it is the hot thing that acts."

Subsistence Of The Soul According To Plato And Aristotle

Did St. Thomas regard his doctrine of the subsistence
of the human soul as a new philosophical view? Quite the
contrary. He claimed that the later Greek philosophers were
aware of the independence of the soul in its operation and
that they concluded from this that the intellective part of the
soul is a self-subsisting thing. The philosophers he had in mind
are obviously Plato and Aristotle, to whom in fact he refers.
Aristotle, he states, says in the *De anima* that the intellect is
a substance, and is not corrupted. The reference may be to *De
anima*, I, 4 (408b 18-19): "The case of mind is different; it
seems to be an independent substance implanted within the
soul and to be incapable of being destroyed." The statement
could also refer at least indirectly to the famous passage in *De
anima*, III, 5 (430a 14-20) where Aristotle distinguished the

two intellects, one passive, the other active, and characterizes the latter as separable, impassible and unmixed.[8] "The teaching of Plato," St. Thomas continues, "who maintains that the soul is immortal and subsists of itself in view of the fact that it moves itself, amounts to the same thing. For he took 'motion' in a broad sense to signify every operation; hence he understands that the soul moves itself because it moves itself by itself." The reference to Plato is evidently to the *Phaedrus*, 245C-246A.

Up to this point, the views of Aristotle and of Plato as understood by St. Thomas are consistent with St. Thomas' contention that the human soul is subsistent. But Plato seems to go beyond this to adopt an extreme view which St. Thomas cannot accept. This is evidently the case in *Alcibiades*, I, 129E-130C. Plato's view of man as stated by Socrates in this dialogue is clear-cut. Man is not the body, nor is he the union of soul and body together. Man is identified with the soul. There is no problem here about the nature of man. Man is a soul. That is his essence. But Plato's view of man creates a problem respecting the body's relation to the essence of man. To exclude the body from man's essence is to reduce it to an accident or at least to a distinct substance whose relation to the soul is merely accidental. Man would be a soul using a body. Here is St. Thomas' statement of the case: "Plato maintained that the human soul not only subsisted of itself, but also had the complete nature of a species. For he held that the complete nature of the [human] species is found in the soul, saying that a man is not a composite of soul and body, but a soul joined to a body in such a way that it is related to the body as a pilot is to a ship, or as one clothed to his clothing."

The Human Soul As Form Of The Body

For St. Thomas this position of Plato is untenable. Aristotle, he thinks, came closer to the truth on this point by

relating the soul to the body as its substantial form. It is in
these terms that St. Thomas himself conceives the nature of
the soul. The human soul is not the essence of man. Rather,
it is constitutive of the essence inasmuch as it is the form of
the body.

How is this to be demonstrated? The steps in the argument bring out some of the metaphysical depths of the Thomistic notion of the human soul. In the argument, St. Thomas
links the concept of the *soul* with the concept of *form* by
means of the identification of *vivere* (function of soul) and *esse*
(function of form), that is to say, the *act of living* and the *act
of existing*. The logic of the argument moves swiftly and forcefully. Let us state the argument in this way:

The soul is that which gives life to the body.

Now the act of living (*vivere*) is the act of existing (*esse*) of
living things.

Consequently the human soul is that which gives the body
its act of existing.

Now the form is precisely that which gives the act of existing.

Therefore the human soul is the form of the body.

To this argument, St. Thomas subjoins some specific
reasons why the soul cannot be in the body as a pilot in a ship.
First, he argues, if this were so, then the soul would give
neither the body nor its parts their specific nature. In fact,
however, the body is a human body and the arms and legs are
human arms and legs owing to the vitalizing presence of the
soul. We see this clearly when we consider the contrary condition of the body and its parts. As St. Thomas says, "when the
soul leaves the body, the body's individual parts retain their
original names only in an equivocal sense. For the eye of a
dead man, like the eye of a portrait or that of a statue, is called
an eye equivocally; and similarly for the other parts of the
body." "Furthermore," St. Thomas adds, "if the soul were in
the body as a pilot in a ship, it would follow that the union
of soul and body would be an accidental one. Then death,

which brings about their separation, would not be a substantial corruption; which is clearly false."

Manifestly, for St. Thomas, man is a substantial unit, a substantial composite of soul and body, not an accidental unity of two substances.

The Human Soul As Hoc Aliquid

At this point, St. Thomas seems to draw his main conclusion. The remarkable thing is that it is a most remarkable conclusion. While using Aristotelian concepts all through the article, he understands them in a way which permits him to reach a conclusion that clearly surpasses Aristotle's thought, if not even contradicts it. In Aristotle, there is no question but that the human soul is conceived as the form of the body. Forms for Aristotle are drawn from the potency of matter and through substantial or accidental change are reduced to the potency of matter. They do not exist apart from matter. That intellective part of the soul which is said to be "what it is by virtue of making all things" is characterized as "separable, impassible, unmixed." This text is subject to various interpretations. Whatever it may mean, clearly Aristotle does not identify form with the individual in the genus of substance, which is what St. Thomas understands by the expression *hoc aliquid*.

But St. Thomas does this very thing. The human soul is the form of the body. At the same time it is a *hoc aliquid*; it is this particular thing — *et sic simul est forma et hoc aliquid*. How in the eyes of St. Thomas is it possible to make this identification? Previously in this article, St. Thomas had already identified the human soul with form. He repeats this identification at this point of the article. It is *forma corporis*. If at the same time, the soul is also *hoc aliquid*, in what precise sense is it *hoc aliquid*? St. Thomas explains that it is an *hoc aliquid* inasmuch as it exists of itself — *anima est hoc aliquid ut per se subsistens*. Does this mean that the human soul by itself, apart from the body, comprises the human species? If so, then we are back with Plato who identifies man with the soul. St. Thomas rejected this view of Plato on the grounds that the soul is the form of the body. As form of the body it cannot by itself comprise the species *man*. Yet as a *hoc aliquid*, it must have its own species.

St. Thomas here appears to be caught in a dilemma. The mark of a profound thinker surely lies in his ability to make proper distinctions. St. Thomas dispels the dilemma here by drawing an important distinction which, if correct, would indicate a profundity of insight over that of Aristotle. The distinction he makes is that between a thing which has a complete species of its own, that is, which lacks nothing so far as its being the kind of thing it is is concerned, and a thing which does not have a complete species of its own but which in some manner completes the human species by being the form of the body.[9] It is in this way that the human soul is both form and *hoc aliquid*. St. Thomas' use of the word *quasi* here seems to suggest that this is a unique case and that there is no real basis for comparison by which we are to understand it. Indeed, if it is a unique case, it is so simply because man himself is a unique reality, being neither a material composite of matter and form nor an immaterial spirit of pure form but a being who is almost a pure spirit so far as existence goes but at the same time truly animal so far as the complete operation of his species goes. In other words, man is an "incarnate spirit" or perhaps, more accurately, a spirit-endowed-animal.[10]

St. Thomas' Argument

Evidently, St. Thomas himself realized that this conclusion identifying the soul as both form and a particular thing (*hoc aliquid*) is a challenging one, not readily grasped by everyone. For this reason, he was not content to rest his case with drawing the conclusion. He went on to subjoin a direct demonstration of the conclusion.

The conclusion, in his view, can be seen from a consideration of the order found among natural forms. His characterization of the hierarchy of forms reflects the perspective of the physics of his day. These descriptions, however, appear to be incidental rather than essential to the reality of the grades of being found among forms.

The general metaphysical principle determining the hierarchy of corporeal forms is this: the higher the form, the more it resembles and approaches higher principles.[11] The truth of this can be observed from the proper operations of forms. St. Thomas then proceeds to distinguish five grades of forms, extending from the forms of elements, which are nearest to matter and devoid of any operation surpassing material dispositions, to the forms which are human souls. Intervening in the hierarchy are the forms of minerals (mixed bodies), the forms which are the souls of plants and the forms which are the souls of animals, manifesting an ascending order of less materiality and greater immanence in their operations, thereby bearing a closer resemblance to the pure intelligences which in ancient physical theory accounted for the movement of the heavenly bodies.

The highest among the forms of bodies are the human souls which bear a more perfect resemblance to the superior substances, that is, the pure intelligences or angels. Human souls, on the one hand, resemble the pure intelligences inasmuch as they are capable in their intellectual activity of knowing immaterial things, while, on the other hand, they differ from pure intelligences inasmuch as this intellectual knowledge of immaterial things must naturally be acquired from the knowledge of material things gained through the senses.

Thus human souls at one and the same time are both similar to and different from the superior substances or pure intelligences. They are similar in that they are capable of the immaterial activity of intellectual knowledge. But this similarity is deeper still. On the principle that a thing's mode of operation is proportionate to its mode of existence, if human

souls resemble pure intelligences in their mode of operation,
they must resemble them also in their mode of existence. In
other words, human souls must be capable of existing independently of the body. But this resemblance is not complete. For
human souls cannot naturally acquire their intellectual knowledge except through the senses which operate conjointly with
the body. What follows? Simply this, that the human soul
cannot be complete as to its species except through its union
with the body, since a thing's species is complete only if it
possesses the things necessary for the proper operation of its
species. It thus appears that the human soul is complete as to
its existence, since it is a form capable of existing apart from
the body. Yet it is incomplete in its species as to its operation,
since it is incapable of exercising completely the operation
proper to its species except in union with the body. In summary, then, we may say that the human soul is a form which
is a *hoc aliquid* but a *hoc aliquid* which apart from the body is
incomplete in its species.

   With respect to the purely spiritual realm of beings and
the purely corporeal realm, where does this view of St. Thomas
situate the human soul? Let us permit St. Thomas to answer
in his words: "if the human soul, inasmuch as it is united as
form to the body, has an act of existing which transcends the
body and does not depend on it, obviously the soul itself is
established on the boundary line dividing corporeal from separate substances — *ipsa est in confinio corporalium et separatarum
substantiarum constituta.*

The Uniqueness Of Man's Soul And Of Man

   Suppose one agrees with St. Thomas that the soul has a
complete act of existing of its own, what seems to follow from
this position? Simply that the body is united to the soul accidentally. For whatever accrues to a thing after it has its complete substantial being, is an accident of that thing, as whiteness and clothing are accidents of man. This precisely is the

position taken by the first objection in the article we have been analyzing. How does St. Thomas reply to this objection? He gives two reasons why it does not follow that the body is united to the soul accidentally.

First, it does not follow, because the same act of existing that belongs to the soul is conferred on the body—*communicatur corpori*—by the soul so that there is one act of existing for the whole composite. Here St. Thomas indicates the uniqueness of the human soul as form of the body. In the doctrine of Aristotle, it is neither the form nor the matter that exists, but the whole composite. This would seem to apply to the human soul as it does to other forms. But not for St. Thomas. For him, the human soul is a different sort of form, namely, a subsistent form which is not only capable of existing independently of the body but also, when united to the body, communicates its existence to the body in such a way that the human body exists, not simply by the existence of the composite but by the existence communicated to it by the human soul.

Secondly, the union is not accidental, because, while the soul can subsist of itself, it does not have a complete species, for the soul needs the body in order to complete man's species —*corpus advenit ei ad completionem speciei*. In other words, in the teaching of St. Thomas, the complete species, man, is a substantial composite of body and soul, not the soul alone, since the soul cannot exercise all the operations proper to the human species without the body.

Even if one were unable to accept this concept of man and of the human soul, one would be compelled to admire the ingenuity exercised by St. Thomas in forging all the conflicting elements deriving from Plato and Aristotle and the Christian faith into a consistent and cogent explanation of both the substantial unity of man as a composite of body and soul related in terms of matter and form and the unique character of the human soul as a subsistent form complete as to independent existence but needing to communicate its existence to the body in order to complete the species of man.

III. THE ORIGIN OF MAN
AND OF THE HUMAN SOUL

The Origin of Man

But if man is such a composite of spirit informing matter, how is one to explain the origin of this uniquely complex being straddling the world of bodies and the world of pure spirits? Is man's location at the intersection of two different worlds to be accounted for by an ascent from below or by a descent from above? Evidently, neither the contemporary concept of man as "the naked ape" nor the Cartesian concept of man as "an angel driving a machine" can serve as models for answering the question. If man is truly the kind of being we have found described in the writings of St. Thomas, it seems reasonable to consult those writings further for possible enlightenment on man's origin.

From the approach in his treatment of the human soul in the *Summa contra gentiles* where the human soul is identified as an intellectual substance united to a body, one can immediately surmise the probable direction of St. Thomas' thinking about the origin of the human soul. There is no need for guesswork, however, since St. Thomas expressly treats of the origin of man's soul and body in questions ninety and ninety-one of the *Summa theologiae*, Part One.

In discussing this question, it is necessary to locate it within the general background of the treatise on creation.[12] Man, like all other finite beings, is a creature and like all creatures owes his first beginning to the creative act of God. Whatever room there may be in the doctrine of St. Thomas for development among finite beings, there is no question in his mind that God is the absolutely First Cause of the universe. By the time he comes to treat of the first production of man's soul and body in questions ninety and ninety-one, the question of the absolute origin of the universe by creation is already a settled question.

The Origin Of The Human Soul

But while the question of man's absolute origin easily fits into the context of the universal creation of all things by God, the precise question of the origin of the human soul is not so simply settled within the framework of the principles of St. Thomas' philosophy. The reason is that forms do not ordinarily come into being through a direct creative act, and according to the teaching of St. Thomas the human soul, as we have seen, is considered to be the form of the body. How then can its coming to be be explained by creation? In the metaphysics of the Angelic Doctor, coming to be or to be made is the way to existence and for this reason a thing must be made in such a way as is suitable to its manner of existence. Now what is it that properly speaking exists except that which itself has its own existence, which has existence in its own right, which subsists, that is, as a substance? That is why only substances are properly and truly called beings. An accident, on the other hand, does not have existence in its own right but is called a being in the sense that something which it qualifies is said to be by it, as, for instance, whiteness is called a being, because by it something is white. Hence an accident rightly is said to be *of being* rather than to be *a being*.

Now this condition applies to all forms and not only to accidental forms. It does not belong to form as such to be made; rather, forms are said to be made through the composite substances being made of which they are forms. If the human soul is the form of the body, how then can it be said to be made or created? Like other forms, it would seem to come into being either through the alteration of the substance as in the case of an accidental form or through the generation of the substance as in the case of a substantial form.

This would normally be true even for the human soul. Like other substantial forms, it would come into being through the generation of a new substance, that is to say, through a substantial change. If there is an exception, it is owing to a

major difference which we have seen St. Thomas ascribe to
the human soul. The human soul is not simply a form; it is a
subsistent form; indeed, it is a particular thing, a *hoc aliquid*.
As a subsistent form, it is proper for it both to be and to be
made.[13] But how will it be made? Can it be produced from pre-
existing matter? To be produced from pre-existing matter, it
would have to exist potentially in the matter and what is
more, it would have to be a corporeal form. But what if the
human soul is a spiritual form? Since spirit and matter are ex-
clusive as to their very nature and belong to irreducible orders
of being, there can be no potentiality within matter to be ele-
vated to the spiritual order of being. As St. Thomas declares:
"For an act to be produced from the potentiality of matter is
nothing else but that something becomes actual which previously was in potentiality. But since the rational soul does
not depend in its existence on corporeal matter, and is subsistent, and exceeds the capacity of corporeal matter, it is not
educed from the potentiality of matter"—*non educitur de potentia materiae.*[14] That the human soul exceeds the capacity of
matter is a strong conviction of St. Thomas based upon an
analysis of its intellectual operations which he finds to be intrinsically immaterial operations.

Having excluded also the possibility of the soul being
produced from some sort of spiritual matter, the firm conclusion drawn by St. Thomas from these considerations of the nature of the human soul is that it can only come into being
through an act of creation—*necesse est dicere quod non fiat nisi
per creationem.*[15] For being a subsistent form, as has been said,
it properly belongs to the human soul to be and to be made.
What is more, since creation is exclusively a divine act which
presupposes nothing pre-existing whereas production by a second agent consists only in changing some pre-existing matter,
God alone, without any intervening created agent, immediately creates the human soul which, not existing potentially
in matter, cannot come into being through a mere substantial
change.[16]

In his *De potentia*, q. 3, a. 9, St. Thomas considers at some length the possibility of man's soul being propagated through corporeal generation from the seed produced in sexual intercourse. The exclusion of this possibility is based on the contention, first, that the human soul, unlike other forms, is a subsistent immaterial form incapable of being produced from any pre-existing entity (*non potest fieri ex aliquo*); secondly, that the action of a corporeal power cannot be raised to the level of causing a thoroughly spiritual and incorporeal active principle such as the rational soul, since no agent is effective beyond the limits of its specific nature (*nihil enim agit ultra suam speciem*); thirdly, that, whereas all forms coming to be through generation are brought forth from the potency of matter, the rational soul which has activities in which the body is not involved cannot be propagated by way of generation (*anima rationalis non propagetur per virtutem generantis*). The conclusion stated at the close of the first argument holds equally for all three arguments, namely, that the rational soul comes into existence through an act of creation as though made out of nothing (*Unde restat quod exeat in esse per creationem, quasi ex nihilo facta*).

Twofold Source Of Man's Origin

Granting that the human soul does in fact owe its origin, not to the power of generation residing in human parents but to a direct creative act of God, what do the parents contribute to the production of man? Can human nature even be said to be passed on from parent to child? There seems to be no question in the mind of St. Thomas that human nature is truly derived from parent to child, although the derivation is necessarily limited to the corporeal side of human nature.[17] In his eyes, it is not possible that a subsistent form such as the human soul, which does not depend for existence upon its union with the body, owe the cause of its existence to the generating act of parents. In the unique case of the human soul it suffices that the act of generation be the cause of the union of such a form with matter by disposing the matter for the form, without being the cause of the form itself.[18]

The result of this twofold source of human origin is not that the body and the soul possess a twofold existence in man, one acquired by the body from the parents, another derived by the soul from the Creator. It is rather that the Creator gives existence to the soul in the body while generation by the parents disposes the body to participate in this existence through the soul united to it.[19] St. Thomas does not see any difficulty in this arrangement. Of course, it would not be possible for two entirely different agents to cooperate in such a way that the action of the one would terminate at the matter and the action of the other at the form. But this could happen in the case of two coordinated agents, one of whom would be the instrument of the other. For the action of the principal agent sometimes extends to something to which the action of the instrument cannot extend. Now nature in relation to the power of God is like an instrument. For this reason there is nothing unsuitable for the divine power alone to cause the rational soul and for the action of nature to extend solely to the disposing of the body.[20]

In the following article of the De potentia (a. 10), St. Thomas confirms his position that the human soul is created in the body and not apart from or before the body. These latter would make the union of body and soul an accidental rather than a substantial union and would require that human souls, not being individuated through matter, be specifically different from one another. Besides, the rational soul, being also sensitive and vegetative, could not suitably be created apart from the body, nor would there be any reason for its union with the body if a separate existence were natural to it.[21]

Other considerations about the production of the human soul, such as the time of its infusion into the body or the possible evolution of the body to a perfection proportioned to the perfection of the soul informing it are secondary considerations and not essential to the very concept of man. St. Thomas himself argued that the first body of man was formed by God without intermediary agents—*necesse fuit quod primum corpus hominis immediate formaretur a Deo.*[22] On the other hand, he thought that in the generation of other individual human beings, the body of man, through a series of generations and corruptions, becomes informed by a succession of vital principles prior to receiving a human soul which comes, not by way of generation, but through a direct act of creation by God.[23]

In view of the more advanced knowledge of contemporary embryology which favors the presence of human life at a much earlier stage than was currently thought in the thirteenth century, St. Thomas, if alive today, would probably have some second thoughts about the time of the infusion of the human soul. It would only be speculation to try to speak for him in the circumstances of present-day scientific knowledge on this important issue. But whatever he has said or would say on the question of the time of creation of the human soul is not essential to the vision of man's nature and of man's ultimate origin bequeathed to us by the Angelic Doctor.

IV. CONCLUSION: EVOLUTION CANNOT EXPLAIN MAN'S TOTAL BEING

The essential thing about man is his unique nature as spirit enfleshed, a being akin to the earth as partaking of its common clay and at the same time similar to angelic natures as sharing with them intelligence and freedom. Long before Pascal and his *Pensées*, St. Thomas saw that man's greatness lies in his power of thought. Even the roots of his liberty are imbedded in reason.[24] Yet intelligence itself is but a sign of the underlying spiritual dimension in man. It is because of this spiritual dimension that man is a person. Intellectual natures, according to St. Thomas, are much more like whole entities than other natures.[25] It is no wonder, then, that man is of more value than many sparrows.[26] Although he walks the earth with other animals, he walks erect on two legs with his head held high toward the heavens in the direction of his deepest strivings and aspirations. There is discernible in man in all his endeavors at least a faint nostalgia for something beyond the earth's horizon. St. Thomas' concept of man reveals the reason why. It is because man bears within the essential structure of his being a component which does not arise from the earth. Through man, spirit has entered the world of bodies but it has entered from a transcendent realm. For this reason, man's total being is inexplicable in terms of a cosmic development.

St. Thomas did not have to face the questions of today's paleontologists as do today's Thomists. No doubt, he would have been open to the new problems as he was open to the speculations current in his day. But regardless of the transmutations that may possibly have prepared the human body, it is the presence of the human soul that from the moment of man's first appearance makes such a body to be a human body. And insofar as this inner principle of man is an intellectual substance, the origin of man in the concept of St. Thomas will always appear more like a descent from the angel than an emergence from the beast. As a major witness to this transcendent source of human dignity, Thomism stands as a safeguard against any degradation of man.

Center for Thomistic Studies
University of St. Thomas

NOTES

1. Restricted by its empirical method, a scientific theory of human evolution is unable to discover a spiritual dimension in man. Hence by the very nature of things, when such a theory becomes confused with a philosophy, the resulting concept of man will inevitably be materialist. Article two of *Humanist Manifesto II* exemplifies this: "Modern science discredits such historic concepts as the 'ghost in the machine' and the 'separable soul.' Rather, science affirms that the human species is an emergence from natural evolutionary forces." The philosophical conclusion drawn from this statement is that "the total personality is a function of the biological organism." On the other hand, the same result does not necessarily follow when evolution is conceived as a genuine philosophical principle as in the philosophy of Bergson.

2. The striking resemblances between animal "intelligence" and human intelligence observed in recent studies of chimpanzees and gorillas are not conclusive enough to abolish the specific difference between man and beast. For an interesting article on these studies, see: R. J. McLaughlin, "Language and Man: Aristotle Meets Koko," *The Thomist*, 45 (1981): 541-570. Darwin himself thought that the fact of man being a moral being capable of reflecting on his past actions and their motives "is the greatest of all distinctions between him and the lower animals." *The Descent of Man*, Chap. 21, *Great Books Of The Western World* (Chicago, London, Toronto: Encyclopaedia Brittanica, Inc., 1951), Vol. 49, p. 592. At the same time, Darwin regarded the mental powers of the higher animals to be the same in kind with those of man, differing only in degree. *Op. cit.*, p. 591.

3. Jacques Maritain proposed that St. Thomas, who, he says, did not have the idea of what we today call Evolution, has given us in advance (*Summa contra gentiles*, III, 22—hereafter SCG) the true basis of the philosophy of Evolution as well as the metaphysical principles of a thought in reality evolutionist. See his *Approches Sans En-*

traves (Paris: Fayard, 1973), p. 112. Not everyone, however, shares
with Maritain this interpretation of the dynamic character of Thomistic metaphysics. Fr. Nogar, for example, who was evidently interested in the undeveloped possibilities of Thomism, nevertheless
regarded St. Thomas as "precipitously caught up by the transhis-
torical" and saw in his doctrine a serious "failure of space-time
orientation." As a result, acccording to Nogar, "in every area of
Thomistic tradition, whether it be about the cosmos, man, or God,
the thought labors under the myopic, static, deterministic fixity of
'the eternal return.'" Raymond J. Nogar, "Aquinas, Sartre, and the
Lemmings" in John N. Deely and Raymond J. Nogar, *The Problem
of Evolution* (New York: Appleton-Century-Crofts, 1973), pp. 371,
372, and note 1, p. 374.

In his *The Wisdom of Evolution* (Garden City, New York:
Doubleday, 1963), Fr. Nogar examined the philosophical and theological implications of the scientific "fact" of evolution. While
biologists, he affirmed elsewhere, no longer question the prehistoric
fact of organic evolution, Nogar himself distinguished several meanings of "fact," pointing out that the statement "evolution is a fact"
remains *in the order of probability*, not *in the order of certainty*. See his
Evolutionism, Its Power and Limits (Washington, D.C.: The Thomist
Press, 1964), pp. 20, 16. See also his article "The Darwin Centen-
nial: A Philosophical Intrusion," *The New Scholasticism*, 33 (1959):
411-445. The effect of Fr. Nogar's studies, according to Deely (*The
Problem of Evolution*, p. ix), was to bring some Christian thinkers to
"acknowledge the power of evolutionary thought."

Robert T. Francoeur, *Perspectives In Evolution* (Baltimore-
Dublin: Helicon Press, 1965), pp. 40, 249-253, detects a dichotomy
between St. Thomas' "dynamic" metaphysics which "calls out for
an evolutionary interpretation and world vision" and his "static"
philosophy of nature. Resolution of the problem, for Francoeur,
seems to require, after the manner of Teilhard de Chardin, the sub-
stitution of a "philosophy of becoming" for a "philosophy of being"
(op. cit., pp. 255, 257), which, of course, would be a metamorphosis
insufferable to Thomism, if not even superfluous for a metaphysics
that is already "dynamic."

Another recent effort to explore the theological and philosophical implications of evolution will be found in Bernard Ryan,
F.S.C., Ph. D., *The Evolution of Man* (Westminster, Maryland: The
Newman Press, 1965). This work and the works already cited provide a partial bibliography on this question.

4. *De moribus ecclesiae*, I, 27, Migne, *Patrologia Latina*, 32: 1332.

5. I am passing over here some obscurities in Aristotle's notion of the soul. In what sense is the separate mind a part of the soul for Aristotle? The soul, as the actuality of matter, cannot exist separately from matter. On the other hand, its intellectual activity demands a principle of action that has separate existence. The Aristotelian texts do not provide a satisfactory solution to these difficulties. Cf. Joseph Owens, C.Ss.R., *A History Of Ancient Western Philosophy* (New York: Appleton-Century-Crofts, 1959), p. 321.

6. *Nec etiam in ejus propria operatione possibile est communicare aliquod organum corporale, ut sit aliquod corporeum organum intelligendi, sicut oculus est organum videndi.* All the Latin texts from this article are quoted from: *St. Thomas Aquinas Quaestiones De Anima*, edited by James H. Robb (Toronto: Pontifical Institute Of Mediaeval Studies, 1968), Quaestio Prima.

7. *Sic oportet quod anima intellectiva per se agat, utpote propriam operationem habens absque corporis communione.*

8. Other possible references in Aristotle's *De anima*: II, 1, 413 a 49; II, 2, 413 b 24-29; III, 4.

9. *Non quasi habens in se completam speciem, sed quasi perficiens speciem humanam ut est forma corporis.*

10. The apt phrase for expressing the uniquely complex nature of the human being eludes the tongue. Anton Pegis used the phrase "incarnated spirit." James Robb employed the phrase "infinite spirit." Not everyone is comfortable with these appellations on account of their Platonic overtones. See: Anton C. Pegis, *At the Origins of the Thomistic Notion of Man* (New York: The Macmillan Company, 1963), p. 46; James H. Robb, *Man As Infinite Spirit* (Milwaukee: Marquette University Publications, 1974).

11. *Invenitur enim inter formas inferiorum corporum tanto aliqua altior quanto superioribus principiis magis assimilatur et appropinquatur.*

12. *ST*, I, 44-49.

13. *Anima autem rationalis est forma subsistens: unde ipsi proprie competit esse et fieri. ST*, I, 90, 2.

14. *ST*, I, 90, 2 ad 2.

15. *ST*, I, 90, 2.

16. *Et quia anima rationalis non potest produci per transmutationem alicujus materiae, ideo non potest produci nisi a Deo immediate. ST*, I, 90, 3. The incongruity of the Thomist concept of man with pure Darwinism is here put in strong relief. There is no evident room

in Darwin's conception of man for a direct divine action. "He who is not content to look, like a savage, at the phenomena of nature as disconnected," Darwin wrote, "cannot any longer believe that man is the work of a separate act of creation." *Descent of Man,* Chap. 21, Great Books, Vol. 49, p. 590.

17. *Humana autem natura traducitur a parente in filium per traductionem carnis. De potentia,* 3, 9 ad 3.

18. *Tunc sufficit quod generans sit causa unionis talis formae ad materiam per hoc quod disponit materiam ad formam; nec oportet quod sit causa ipsius formae. De potentia,* 3, 9 ad 6.

19. *De potentia,* 3, 9 ad 20.

20. *De potentia,* 3, 9 ad 21.

21. *De potentia,* 3, 10.

22. *ST,* I, 91, 2.

23. *De potentia,* 3, 9 ad 9; SCG, II, 89, [11]: *ST,* I, 118, 2 ad 2; *ST,* I, 76, 3 ad 3.

24. *Unde totius libertatis radix est in ratione constituta. De veritate,* 24, 2.

25. *Naturae autem intellectuales maiorem habent affinitatem ad totum quam aliae naturae: nam unaquaeque intellectualis substantia est quodammodo omnia, inquantum totius entis comprehensiva est suo intellectu.* SCG, III, 112.

St. Thomas Aquinas and Husserl On Intentionality

Anton C. Pegis

I

I shall try in two lectures to cover the topic of intentionality (which is much better understood if approached indirectly) in two thinkers: St. Thomas Aquinas and Edmund
Husserl, the founder of modern phenomenology. Husserl had
an illustrious pupil and competitor, Martin Heidegger, who
went his own way, and perhaps was not a true follower of
phenomenology; I'm going to give only incidental references
to Heidegger.

Mainly, I shall be concerned simply with the Husserl
who is the founder of transcendental phenomenology, that is,
only with the Husserl who wrote *The Idea of Phenomenology*
(1907), *Ideas*, (only the first volume of which appeared in
England in 1913), and *The Paris Lectures*, which he later re-
vised and published as the *Cartesian Meditations*. I would have
liked to include the Husserl who wrote his last "Introduction
to Phenomenology," (He was always writing them—every one
of the titles I have mentioned has the subtitle "Introduction
to Phenomenology." Husserl claimed he was always a "begin-
ner.") The last such Introduction he wrote was *The Crisis*,
which was published in 1936. It is not as engaging a work as
the earlier ones. Husserl was now old and worried both by the
appearance of logical positivism in Vienna and also by the activity of Heidegger, by his pulling phenomenology in the

direction of existentialism. At least that is how Husserl described it. And he wondered during the last years of his life whether there was still room for a phenomenology between existentialism, on the one hand, and logical positivism, on the other. Well, there was, and there still is. That will be the Husserl I shall be concerned with, and alongside him I should like to deal with St. Thomas Aquinas, and examine what he has to say about knowledge, and to compare the two, or rather, try to understand from two different points of view the notion of intentionality.

Husserl and Aquinas: Historical Background

Husserl and Aquinas are separated by 700 years; their interests are different, their backgrounds are different, and between them there stand two revolutionary thinkers, namely, Descartes and Kant. The former was at the origin of Husserl's twentieth-century Cartesianism, as Husserl himself called it; the latter, Kant, was the teacher of Husserl's final steps in idealism. The question now arises: If a Husserl who could inaugurate his whole philosophy without the Cartesian "cogito" is unthinkable, how can I usefully compare him with St. Thomas, who obviously did not know the "cogito"; and from the point of view of the exposition of his thought, did not need it?

There is an answer to that question, and it is a twofold one. One part of it is historical, the other doctrinal. The historical part is not particularly difficult to discover. St. Thomas' conception of knowledge, as we shall see, is fundamentally Aristotelian. He took from Aristotle's *De anima* his explanation of the phenomenon we call human knowledge. Moreover, as we shall see, he drew from the *Metaphysics* his general analysis of action and of knowing which, following Aristotle, he called immanent action. He was particularly Aristotelian in his view of knowledge as a living phenomenon. Human knowing was certainly a mystery. In an entirely mysterious way, the human intellect, by its own being, comes to be the known thing, and both the becoming and the subsequent being of the known thing by the intellect has been associated in Aristotelianism with the notion of intentionality. Intentionality accounts, at least in St. Thomas' eyes, for the phenomenon of knowing as he understood it. The notion is elusive and I must come back to it more than once.

Now, in the second half of the nineteenth-century, there lived a German Aristotelian scholar by the name of Franz Brentano, who revived the notion of intentionality in his work: *Psychology from the Empirical Standpoint*, which he published in 1874. He had learned that notion from Aristotle, and Husserl, in turn, learned it from him. The intentional nature of knowing, whatever be its meaning, unites St. Thomas and Husserl in a common origin and tradition, namely, Aristotelianism. Our problem lies in this starting point. But between St. Thomas and Husserl there stands Descartes, and particularly Descartes' "cogito," which is a methodical starting point for the constitution of a certain philosophy. Now, there is no easy way—I wish there were—to describe what Husserl did (and which is part of our problem), namely the blending of Aristotelian intentionality and the Cartesian "cogito" into a single doctrine. Instead of looking for an easy way, I would like, with your indulgence, to make the description more difficult both in order to be more faithful, and also in order to have the problem adequately before us.

Husserl's Blending of Intentionality with Cartesian "Cogito"

Now, the "cogito" of Descartes is a methodic isolation of the thinking self from the world, although that isolation occurs within the world. It is an exclusion of the world from thought. On the other hand, intentionality is a world-centered view of the human consciousness. As Brentano kept saying, and Husserl kept repeating, "consciousness is consciousness of something." In other words, consciousness is relational, and its very life is expressed in this relation to the world. Let me put this differently. The "cogito" is methodically solitary and subjectivist; intentionality is, let us say, trans-subjective. The "cogito" is centered in thought, even isolated thought; intentionality is centered in the world, that is, in the presence of the world within the consciousness. How can a doctrine that excludes the world—the "cogito"—blend with a doctrine that is centered in the world? Surely it is not an easy position to see; yet Husserl did blend them, and, as they say in one of those old Latin aphorisms, "*Ab esse ad posse valet illatio,*" ("it is quite permissible to infer possibility from existence"). In any case, since Husserl did, in fact, blend them, it must be possible; and yet I don't quite believe it. Because, though we admit he did it, and we shall see so in detail, yet we are permitted to ask the price that he paid for the blending. The outcome of his effort is clear enough (at least it can be formulated simply): it is the transformation of phenomenology specifically into a transcendental idealism. The price? I shall be anticipating no Husserlian secrets if I say the price is precisely what happens to the world and, with the world, to intentionality in Husserl's transcendental phenomenology. Comparing St. Thomas and Husserl, I wish to see what each of them did with his Aristotelian inheritance. How did intentionality function in the theory of knowledge that each man had? Indeed, what did intentionality mean? If, as is the case, St. Thomas' theory of knowledge is realistic, then we must ask what intentionality is, if it can function in a realistic epistemology in St. Thomas, on the one hand, and in an idealistic epistemology in Husserl, on the other. How can intentionality, one and the same doctrine, function in both ways?—which is another way of coming to the question: what does it mean?

Intentionality in Aristotle

Well, there is only one proper way in which to begin the examination of the problem. And certainly that way is not to begin by a comparison of St. Thomas and Husserl; it is by seeing the doctrine of intentionality as it first arose in Aristotle, when, after criticizing the Platonic doctrine of ideas, in a devastating description (*Metaphysics*, I, 9), he was then called upon in his turn, after his rejection of Plato, to explain what the human intellect knew, what its objects of knowledge were, if there were no Platonic ideas to be known, and if intellectual knowing was not, as Plato held, a kind of intuition or vision. And this is the proper point at which to begin our discussion, because we shall not understand the Aristotelian alternative unless we understand first what it is that Aristotle rejected. What did he reject?

To put it briefly, he rejected not only the Platonic metaphysics of a separate world of forms or beings, but along with it he rejected the Platonic epistemology. Now if there is anything that is characteristic of the Platonic epistemology, it is that knowing consists in a vision of what is present. "Vision" and "presence" are two dominating words in Plato's theory of knowledge. The ideas existing in themselves are the intelligibles that the mind of man sees—obscurely, distantly, but sees, and always aims at seeing. And, moreover, the mind sees them inasmuch as they are present. It is an extraordinary experience, at least to me, in reading the middle books of the *Republic*, to recognize, and then to collect information, to be sure of it: how many verbs of seeing there are in that text describing knowledge. To know is to see, but to see what? To see something that is present, that is *there*, there to be seen. The Platonic theory of knowledge is a ladder of vision all the way to the top of being; this is what the sixth and seventh books of the *Republic* indicate. In other words, knowing is a visual phenomenon, explained by the presence to the mind, or before the mind, of that which is known, or seen.

The Aristotelian elimination of the ideas as realities, realities in themselves, had one enormous epistemological consequence: for Aristotle, there were no realities present in their intelligibility to be seen by the mind. So, you are bound to ask some questions once you have pushed the Platonic doctrine aside: What did the mind know if there were no ideas or intelligible forms to be known? What, in terms of the human subject, was intellectual knowledge? Clearly, as an activity, it couldn't be vision if there was not a presence there to be seen. Moreover, by what means did the mind work? And, finally, what was knowledge?—These are reasonable questions.

Given that knowing is not seeing, given that there are no present intelligibles functioning as antecedent objects to be seen, the question immediately focuses on knowing as an activity to be explained in terms of the "informing means" of knowing: the activity of knowing and the constitution of the knower. We can arrive at this new result by way of Aristotle's *De anima*, Book III, chapter 8, and then Aquinas' *Commentary* on this shorter chapter. Let me translate the text of the *De anima*, III, 8, 431b 20 to 432a 16.

> Summarizing what we have said about the soul, let us now say again that the soul is, in a way, all beings. The beings (the things that exist, 'onta') are either grasped by the sense, or they are grasped by the intellect, and knowledge is, in a way, the objects of knowledge, and sense perception is sensible objects. How this is so we must inquire. Knowledge and perception are divided according to their objects, the potential according to the potential, the actual according to the actual, and the perceiving and knowing parts of the soul are potentially these things—the one the knowable, the other the perceivable. These objects must be either things themselves or their forms; not things themselves, for it is not the stone that is in the soul, but its form, so that the soul is as is the hand, for the hand is the organ of organs, and the intellect is the form of forms, and sense perception the form of sensible objects. Since, moreover, there exists nothing (as it seems) apart from the extended magnitudes perceived by the sense, the objects of the intellect are found among the forms perceived by the sense, including both what we call abstractions and the dispositions and affections of sensible objects.

May I backtrack a bit and ask you to notice how Aristotle very nicely universalizes himself? Listen to that first sentence: "Since, moreover, there exists nothing apart from bodies in nature (*as it seems*)." As it seems to whom, then? To Aristotle. He is expressing his opinion behind the cover of an "as it seems." Well, we shouldn't object, but at least we can notice that he isn't beyond such tactics. He is saying: "As it seems, there are only bodies in nature existing; therefore, what the mind sees, must be included within the scope of the objects of the senses." That's a straight Aristotelian position, if you like, hiding its colors behind "as it seems."

> And that is why it is the case both that he who is not perceiving anything would not learn or understand any-thing, and that he who is considering anything must at the same time consider some image, for images are like sense perceptions, except that they are without matter. (end of the text as far as I will need it).

Aquinas on Aristotle

Now Aquinas is not unaware of the importance of *De anima*, Book III, chapter 8. As he sees it, the text contains three major points. I am following his *Commentary on the De anima*, Book III, lecture 13 (ed. Pirotta; Marietti, 1959), nn. 787, 789, 791. Point number one. Aristotle agrees with his predecessors that the soul is all things. Everything that exists is either sensible or intelligible. The sense in the soul is in a manner all sensible things; the intellect is all intelligibles. Point number two. Aristotle, however, Aquinas continues, disagrees with his predecessors on *how* the soul is all things. He writes, and I quote,

> He (Aristotle) says, that if the soul is all things, either it must be the knowable and sensible things themselves, as Empedocles held, that we know earth by earth, water by water, and so on, or it must be their forms. Now the soul is not things themselves, as they, the antiqui, held, because the stone is not in the soul, but rather the form of the stone, and in this way we say that the intellect in

act (the actualized intellect) is the intelligible object in
act, insofar as the form of the object is the form of the
intellect in act.

Thirdly, as a final point, according to Aquinas, Aristotle
eliminates the Platonic position. He proves that the intellect
depends on the sense. There are no separate intelligibles for
the intellect to know by itself. Whatever we know is a
physical body, or some aspect of a physical body. Therefore,
what the intellect knows is to be found as a reality among
sensible forms, both mathematical notions, and physical notions. This has two consequences: without the sense a person
cannot acquire new knowledge, nor use old knowledge. Knowing always involves knowing in and through images.

If we follow the drift of this commentary, it is clear that
St. Thomas believes that according to Aristotle, knowledge
takes place somehow by a similitude through a form. What
that means, we shall have to examine. Moreover, knowledge
is solely *of* bodies and of what is *in* bodies, and therefore what
this requires is some doctrine of abstraction in order to show
the origin of intellectual knowledge in the order of sensibility.
Now, this does not say that things, sensible things, cause my
knowledge; no, this says that I know sensible things by an
identity in form with them. Abstraction, therefore, explains
my identity with things. It accounts for my being constituted
as a knower. And since I must be constituted in this identity
with things *before* knowledge can exist, we must be prepared,
I believe, to entertain in St. Thomas a radical idea: the idea,
namely, that abstraction is in principle a *pre-cognitive condition*
subtending the possibility of knowledge.

Knowledge As My Activity

I have come this far, not to sidetrack what I have just
said, but, in order by having said it to call your attention to
something else. It is very easy for Aristotelians, even Thomists, to think of knowledge as somehow originating in abstrac-

tion. Didn't Aquinas just comment on Aristotle to this effect? But things are not so easy. To think of intellectual knowledge only in terms of abstraction is to forget a deeper aspect of knowledge and of knowing. Let us suppose, to use Aristotle's example, that the stone I know is not itself in me, but rather its likeness or form. In other words, I know the stone by being *likened* to it and by expressing it in my knowing. Yet even so, if the likeness comes somehow—let's leave it open—from the stone, the likening activity by which I express and know the stone comes from *me*. The point is that *knowing as an activity* comes from me. It is something that I do. It is my action taking place in me, needing the cooperation of things, as we shall see. But the action of knowing, as an action, comes from me. It is *my* action, and it would be disastrous to forget this side of knowledge.

On the contrary, once we do see that knowing is an activity, an activity that I posit, we begin to ask, well, what kind of an action is it? We obviously must try to grasp and understand knowing as an action before we understand knowing as intentionality. Now, there is in Aristotle a classic distinction between immanent and transitive actions, and that distinction lies at the root of our problem. There are several texts. Let me give you three references of which I shall use only two. They are: *Metaphysics*, IX,6,1048b28-36; IX,8,1050a21-1050b1; XI,9,1065b14-1066a7. As I proceed through the first two of these texts, I shall inflict three or four Greek words on you, which I just want you to have seen. They are not absolutely necessary to my presentation except for one point, namely, I am not sure that it is possible to translate one of them adequately into English. But let me follow Aristotle: "Some actions (*praxes*) are motions (*kineses*), and other actions are energies (*energeiai*), or actualities." I feel almost like Heidegger, who insists that the only way to translate Greek is to talk Greek: you have to translate back into the language in order to understand what is being said. Well, I think *energeia* is one of those words. Thomas Aquinas will get the word *actus* out of this, but as a specific translation of this (and he was just

using a translation) he has *operatio* and *operationes* as distinguished from *motus*. So there are actions and some of them are
"motions" and some of them are "actualizations." If you are
not unhappy with that, I will use it.

Now, Aristotle continues: "Any motion, as an action,
is incomplete." There is an internal piecemeal-ness about it.
"To walk, for example, and to have walked, and in general
to move and to have moved are not," says Aristotle, "given
simultaneously (*hama*). On the other hand, to have seen and
to see and to understand (*noein*) and to have understood
(*nenoeken*) are simultaneously the same thing (*hama to auto*)."

Seeing and understanding are, for Aristotle, examples
of the kind of action that *energeia* is, i.e., actualization, which
is given simultaneously whole; on the other hand, walking,
building, becoming, are examples of motions, i.e., actions that
are spread out in time for their completeness. The aspects of
immanence and transitiveness in action can be seen in that
distinction, when we consider the work that these actions do,
the *ergon*. This work is their end, or their purpose, as actions.
An action, in other words, is realized when it is used or exercised,—"used," the Greek word is *chraonai, chresis*. "Use"
here means what we would call "exercise." In sight as an action, the point is, nothing happens beyond the seeing itself;—
the seeing—is both fulfillment and end. Sight is an immanent
action in Aristotle's analysis. But in building as an action,
there is a product, or an effect, beyond the action of building:
the house built is the end of the action. Building is a transitive action. Here are, then, two ways in which our powers are
fulfilled in action. In immanent action—seeing, for example—
the use of the power to see is itself the fulfillment of the
power. In transitive action, the actuality or fulfillment of the
action lies beyond the use of the power, in the thing made or
done.

This distinction among actions, or between the two general types of action, is based on Aristotle's definition of motion as an action and comes from the *Physics*. There motion
is defined as the actualization of the potential as potential,

that is to say, motion, even in the state of actualization, is semi-potential. Look at *Physics*, III, 1,201a10-11. Motion, as an action, is a process in time, existing, not as a whole, but as a growing development.

Consider now what Aristotle is saying: understanding and perceiving are immanent actions, fulfilled as actions, not by any effect beyond themselves, but by their own actualization within themselves. When you walk, you cover a distance, and when, if you are a carpenter, you build a chair, the chair is there as your "effect." Walking and building, or, to use more general terms, doing and making, are realized in an effect beyond themselves.

When I was writing this, I looked at my pen and asked myself, what kind of action is that? Obviously, it is a transitive action, but if you read a linguist like Noam Chomsky, you are aware both of the making of language, the making of the letters, and how difficult that is, and also of putting down symbols for communication. It seems to me that writing, if one is going to categorize it, is an example, at one and the same time, of both doing and making. When I write, I do it with a view to communicating; I am not thinking of the process itself of having learned how to make the letters and how to relate them to one another; that side of writing is gone; or rather it is not gone. I have simply acquired it; you have acquired it; and we all keep writing and we keep thinking of the doing involved in writing; and yet there is more involved than doing, a making is also involved.

Let us say, then, that walking and building, or more generally, doing and making, as actions, are realized in an effect beyond themselves. And if you ask what is the effect of walking, it is precisely to have covered the ground from A to B. They are transitive actions. Now understanding and perceiving —perceiving by the sense—let us say, more generally, knowing— this class of actions is not like doing and making. In knowing I don't do anything, if walking is a model of doing, that is, if that is the kind of doing I am talking about. And it is quite clear that in knowing I don't make anything. Nor, on the

other hand, is knowing, in its kind as an action, a piecemeal
sort of action. It exists as a whole and all at once.

Well, if knowing is an action, how are we to characterize
it? We would not be inclined to say that in knowing I am
making something, but perhaps, we might be inclined to say,
that in knowing I am *doing* something, and clearly I *am* doing
something if knowing, since the time of Aristotle, is an action, a *praxis*. Now if, following Aristotle, we agree that knowing is *not* a transitive action, and has no effect beyond itself,
can we retain the notion of doing but separate it from the notion of transitiveness and from the correlative notion of an effect? In that event, knowing would be a doing that does not
aim at an effect beyond it; it would be a doing that is termi-
nated within the doing itself.

Knowing Is Being the World I Know

What do I do when I know? There can be only one answer and it is a typical one: by knowing, as an action, what
I do is to be the known thing. In other words, the actualization of the power of knowing, the intellect, consists in being
by its action the known thing. Knowing has no effect; it is itself its own effect. To know, as an action, i.e., as distinguished
from walking as doing, and painting as making, consists in *being the known*. Now this conclusion is surprising in itself, but
it is even more surprising in some of its consequences. We are
now able to say, (maybe somewhat gingerly because we are not
yet accustomed to the idea) that to know, as an action, is *to
be* the known thing.

What I must emphasize is that this "to be" is an action.
It is a performance, an enactment, if I may use such somewhat
misplaced language. My knowing consists in being what I
know. And I am using "being" here with all the verbal force
that Heidegger wants to give it when he says that "Being" is
the first participle—all the other participles get their status
and strength from it. My knowing consists in being what I
know. Being what? Well, being the world that I know. That

is to say, not just seeing it as a presence beyond me, but en-
acting it as a world within me. This may sound like what the
existentialists say, but I mean something specific, and it is not
particularly existentialist.

Being what? I ask. Being the world that I know. By my
immanent action, then, in knowing the world, *I am the world*.
The world lives in me by my action. I do not just see the
world, I enact it, and, if we were to think in terms of moral
problems, as say, St. Augustine did, this is why the world is
so troublesome. It filled his life precisely because he lived it,
he lived it so strenuously. By my immanent action, in knowing the world, I am the world. I do not just see the world, I
enact it.

But, (and the consequences get more surprising) how can
I enact it except by becoming the world in and by my action
of knowing? And how can I become the world unless within,
and by means of, my immanent action, I objectify myself in
the world? And how do I do this unless knowing is a self-
transcending action so that I can say that by my action of
knowing I am *in* the world, I am *the* world?

Knowing As a Self-Transcending Action

Here the complications and the consequences begin to
appear. Knowing is an immanent action completed in itself.
But consider this: to know the world around me is for me to
be the world around me. It is also to objectify myself in the
world so that, by my action of knowng, I *am* the world. And
how can this be, unless, within the immanence of my knowledge I am even there in a condition of self-transcendence? We
are ordinarily accustomed to thinking of ourselves as being
physically in the world; I am here in this room; I am in some
place or other in the world. The world is outside of me, I say,
it is there, and I am not there, I am here, in myself. Now there
is nothing wrong with this view expressed in ordinary language, except that it is a dependent and derivative view. It
does not really describe my basic relationship to the world or

even to myself. Am I here in myself? Certainly, in some sense.
But then, so is the world here with me. It is part of me, present
in my knowledge, so that even when I say I am myself alone,
I am still not without the world. When I distinguish myself
from the world, it is the self that already knows and contains
the world that I say is not the world. Is the world out there?
Yes, in some sense it is. But it is also within me, part of me.
And I am myself across this presence of the world in me and
my presence, by knowledge, in the world.

II

By way of conclusion, I shall deal with two problems:
first, the problem of intentionality, and second, the problem
of realism and idealism. Running across both problems there
will be the question of subjectivity versus trans-subjectivity.
These two topics cover the problem of the meaning of intentionality and the consequent problem whether it is an epistemological notion.

Intentionality According to Husserl

So let us get into our first question: what is intentionality? Now, St. Thomas and Husserl both used this Aristotelian notion in their conception of human knowledge, though
not in the same way or for the same purpose. Consider first
Husserl's use. To Brentano's doctrine of intentionality, he
added the Cartesian "cogito." Indeed, he saw the intentional
structure of consciousness within the framework of the "cogito." Two results followed: consciousness is wholly immanent, which means that the transcendence and the objectivity
of the world are phenomena of and in consciousness. They are
part of the immanent world and life of the self.

The second result was Husserl's critique of Cartesian
transcendental realism as philosophical nonsense. There is no
"beyond" the world of consciousness: Husserl interprets in-

tentionality as pure immanence. This is the point of "bracketing." "Bracketing" makes the world into an absolute phenomenon and uncovers the transcendental ego. From this point of view, let us notice that Husserl interprets intentionality not simply as a non-psychological phenomenon, but also as meaning the total immanence of the known in the knower. It is the knower and not any antecedent world who is the source of what he knows.

As a result, Husserl embarks, (and needs to embark), on an elaborate doctrine of the structure of consciousness, explaining how the world is constituted synthetically by the ego that is at the same time structuring itself. So understood, intentionality is a synthesizing function of pure subjectivity: the "cogito." It is a doctrine not of *knowing* the world but of "making" the world. Husserl credits Descartes with effecting the great shift from naive objectivity—the natural attitude—to transcendental subjectivity. The first and basic certitude after the methodic doubt is the "I am" given in the "cogito." This certitude is prior to the world. In his own meditations, Descartes then went on to prove the existence of the world beyond knowledge, after having first proved the existence of God, and using the divine veracity for this leap beyond the immanence of the thinking self.

But Husserl objects, there is really no way to escape from immanence. Consciousness always functions within itself. The "cogito" cannot transcend the pure immanence of subjectivity. It cannot reach an objectivity beyond itself; it can reach a transcendent only within the immanence of the consciousness, in other words, a world that is simply a part of that consciousness.

Transcendental realism is therefore nonsense according to Husserl, (i.e. methodic nonsense), and the "cogito" is closed in subjectivity. We are here dealing with a "methodic subjectivity." Here at the very least there is a possible question. In interpreting intentionality as a function of the "cogito," and as the synthesizing activity of consciousness, was Husserl not making his doctrine say what perhaps it could not of itself really say, and did not intend to say, that is, could not carry? As used by Husserl, intentionality is a doctrine of what he calls transcendental idealism.

Now Brentano had said that consciousness was consciousness of something. This pointed to the relational structure of the consciousness. It was not idealism; it was an effort to treat psychic events faithfully, which meant principally not to treat them as physical realities. Clearly, Brentano's attitude did not lead to idealism; in principle it said nothing about realism and idealism. Husserl, let us then say, "Cartesianized" intentionality, so that his phenomenology, apart from being, or wishing to be, a transcendental descriptive science, is also, and specifically intends to be, a transcendental idealism. As such, it reflects more the influence of Descartes than that of Brentano.

Knowing According to Aquinas

On the other hand, for St. Thomas, human knowledge has two aspects, namely, "inexistence" (to *inexist*) and objectivity. Knowledge is for him a modification in and of the knower, an inexisting event, or action, or accident. But knowledge as similitude is objectivity; it is my being and thus my expressing the thing known by likeness. Thus, as inexistence, knowledge is the assimilation of the known by the knower. As intentional likeness, it is the assimilation of the knower to the known. As likeness, knowledge is not merely objectivity but objectification. I become the known. Knowing as intentional *is* objectification, which is why I can say that in knowing I am the world. In knowing, not as a modification, but strictly as knowing, I become the world intentionally and I then am the world intentionally or by likeness or assimilation. As St. Thomas sees it, therefore, intentionality is essentially self-objectification of the knowing of the knower in the known. In this sense it is not a doctrine of subjectivity but rather a doctrine of trans-subjectivity. Knowing so understood is as such a self-transcending reality.

We must ask: why did Husserl limit intentionality to subjectivity? Judging by his argument against Descartes, we must
say that it was because he thought of knowledge principally as
being within a subject. Knowing was in the knower as a
modification. Was not Husserl looking at knowledge as inexistence, which, if St. Thomas is right, has nothing to do with
intentionality? Let us then ask a more direct question. Is there
anything in the cognitional, that is, the objectifying presence
of the known in the knower, that limits or even directs the
knower to his subjectivity? The answer seems to be no. Intentionality accomplishes my identification as knower with the
known. How can this be subjectivity? And how can it not be
trans-subjectivity?

The Issue Between Husserl and St. Thomas

Well, then, where does the issue between Husserl and
St. Thomas lie? It lies in the *meaning of intentionality*, and in
its *direction as a doctrine*. Against Descartes, Husserl limits the
knower to what is in his consciousness. He thinks he can
prove that there is no world beyond the knower. The world
is given *in* and *by* the knower. This leads Husserl to his own
idealism. But the question is: How does he know that intentionality is purely subjective? Let us grant to Husserl that there
is no "transcendental realism"—what might be called a "di-
vinely-mediated realism." There is no "beyond knowledge"
in that sense.

But, does the fact that there is no "beyond knowledge"
mean that there is no "beyond" the consciousness? The stu-
dent of St. Thomas is bound to ask this question. To St.
Thomas, knowing is trans-subjective; it is self-transcending
and objectifying, and this is, for him, what intentionality
means. It means not subjectivity, but rather subjectivity
caught up in trans-subjectivity. In knowing, far from being
subjectively limited within myself, I exteriorize myself in what
I know. Thus understood, *knowing is my self-transcending
presence in the world*. Intentionality identifies me *with* the

world, and not the world with me. So much so that there is
no question of a "beyond knowledge." In and by knowing I
am by intentional likeness beyond myself, in the other, i.e.
the world. There is, to be sure, a beyondness in knowledge,
but it is my beyondness in the world.

For St. Thomas, knowing is an activity taking place
within me, the knower, by which I am, though within myself,
still beyond myself. The mystery of knowing is that in knowing, which is an action within me, I am beyond myself by likeness in the world of the known. Again, if with St. Thomas,
we emphasize that intentionality is essentially a doctrine of
self-transcendence, of being in the other, indeed of being *the
other*, we cannot see in the doctrine any vehicle for Cartesian
subjectivity. The center and the focus of intentionality are the
other, not the self. And the point of intentionality is the
transcending objectification of the knowing self in the known,
in the transcending other.

We are now before our main problem. If both Husserl
and Aquinas are agreed on the cognitional identity of man
and the world, the question is, is that identity effected in subjectivity or is it a self-transcending objectivity? Is intentionality part of the methodic subjectivity of Husserl, that is to
say, is it a corrected Cartesianism, or is it, as St. Thomas believes, a self-transcending relation to, and presence in the
other, in the world? We can make a choice at this point if we
are willing to accept Brentano's formula that "consciousness
is consciousness of something." It is a psychic, i.e. a non-
physical relation to the known and functions in that relation.
But if intentionality expresses this relational structure of the
consciousness, this relation to the other, then the point of intentionality is the other to which the consciousness is related.
How then can there be a return to transcendental subjectivity,
as Husserl wishes, when the doctrine of intentionality says
that the consciousness is riveted to the other in its life?

Let us repeat the point. If the center of the knowing life
of the consciousness is its intentional tie to the world, to what
it knows, how can the consciousness return to itself directly?

A world-centered consciousness, a consciousness essentially related (in knowing) to what it knows, cannot return to itself, to its subjectivity, except via the world, that is, reflexively, through and across its relation to the world that it knows. From this point of view can we not say that the "cogito" and intentionality are in fact antithetical doctrines? One is centered in the direct grasp of subjectivity, the other is centered in objectivity, in the other; one grasps the self directly as a consciousness originally present to itself, the other grasps the self reflexively as a consciousness originally present to the world.

In Husserl, the "cogito" subjectivizes and phenomenalizes the world in order to include it. In St. Thomas, intentionality centers the self in a self-transcending identity or relation with the world as its permanent condition. In Husserl, subjectivity constitutes the world in order to account, in the line of the "cogito," for the transcending presence of the world to consciousness. In St. Thomas, the knowing self constitutes its knowing presence in the world, which remains radically other and independent in relation to consciousness.

Can Intentionality Be Combined with the "Cogito"?

If then intentionality, as inherited by Husserl from Brentano, means the self-transcendence and objectification of the knowing self in relation to the otherness of the world, how can it combine with the "cogito" as an expression and vehicle of Husserl's transcendental subjectivity? It seems to me, on straight doctrinal grounds, that it cannot. Yet Husserl did combine them and the question is to know the ground or the basis of the combining. Husserl's "ground" was his aim to modernize Descartes; to expand Descartes' *ego cogito* to *ego cogito cogitata*. Put in terms of his teaching, this means that Husserl made phenomenology into an epistemological doctrine, a transcendental idealism. And yet, why is phenomenology, as an eidetic description of essences, and even of the world as a symbolic carrier of essential relations, an idealistic

[handwritten margin note: That is the phenomenon... Not if we buy]

epistemology? Why is it not, as phenomenology, a return to, and a description of, man's lived world in its experiential and pre-theoretical constitution?

But no, to Husserl phenomenolgy was a theory of knowledge, a transcendental idealism, a reformed cartesianism. Husserl imposed, I believe, a subjectivist epistemology on the meaning of intentionality. The question is then to know whether he succeeded in doing so. This may not be possible to answer. If he was satisfied with the results, why was he not successful in his own eyes? But there is another side to this question. It would not be unfair to ask what happened to the notion of the other, to the world, in Husserl's transcendental idealism? What happened to the world merely as world, objective, transcendent, and self-giving? So far as the world is made of things, each one an individual identity, an *x* as Husserl says, the world is lost after reduction; it is lost as world. By this I mean that it is translated into synthesizing ideas of consciousness "regulating" the continuity of experience. After reduction, in spite of Husserl, in spite of his effort, there is no world. There is transcendent experience and there are ideas guiding its endless unfolding. Reduction as such need not have eliminated the world in phenomenalizing it, but reduction was also an epistemological undertaking. As the first step of such an undertaking, it set out to synthesize the world, not to find it in its transcendence.

Intentionality Is Not an Epistemological Doctrine

I am not concerned here with Husserl's idealism as a philosophical position. Nor am I defending the cause of realism, not just yet. I am simply pointing to the fact that Husserl did use intentionality as an epistemological doctrine. I am therefore saying that intentionality is not of itself an epistemological doctrine, and it is not one for a rather simple reason. It is a description of knowing considered as known. It says that to know is to be the other as other, i.e. to be the other as other by likeness. As a knowing act, we can say that knowing is a self-transcendent identification with the known, with the other, with the world. This is a description or a designation of the act of knowing. Self-transcendence is a characteristic of the act of knowing. To know is to be the other. But this is not an explanation of the other that I am in knowledge. The world transcends me, yet I have been saying that to know the world is to be identified with it. But what am I in the transcendence of the world that knowledge is? In short, a theory of knowledge is called upon to explain my relation to the world that I know.

The data of self-transcendence are the facts with which such a theory begins. The data themselves are not the theory. The data are a first-level phenomenon stemming from knowing as self-transcendence. The theory, whether idealistic or realistic, is a second-level explanation of the intentional data. The first-level fact is that I am in the world in the radical sense of being intentionally identical with it. This is not a theory but a discovery. Just as it is a later recognition that I distinguish myself from the world only within my identity with it. Being in the world is a primitive first-level fact for the human consciousness. When I distinguish myself from the world and think of myself as observing the world and saying that it exists, I am already at a second level of awareness, perhaps what has been called the pre-philosophical awareness of common sense. I am reflecting on and within knowing as self-transcendence, and I am expressing at the level of self-transcendence, reflexively considered, my relations to the world. By this I mean to refer both to the world and to myself.

To sum up, my argument has been limited so far to saying that intentionality as such is not an epistemological doctrine, but a designation of the kind of action that knowing is. I have argued that in using intentionality epistemologically, Husserl lost the notion of the world after reduction and to this extent lost the point of intentionality as a doctrine. It may be true that from an idealistic epistemological standpoint, Husserl retained the world such as he wished to retain it; however, from the point of view of intentionality, he did not retain the world, nor did he retain the notion of knowledge and of the consciousness as a self-transcending relation to the world.

Intentionality is an immanent action whose term is the other, given in and by the action itself, and therefore an objectifying action, centered not in immanence but in transcendence. It is a trans-subjective action in its effect, identifying the consciousness with what it knows. Since, moreover, the focus of intentional being is the other, the known, it follows both that the knower in knowing is in a state of self-transcendence and objectification, and also that the knower is aware of himself only reflexively and secondarily within that transcendence or trans-subjectivity.

Recapitulation and Final Question: Is a Corrected Cartesianism Possible?

The basic starting point for both Husserl and Aquinas was the cognitional identity of man and the world. If that identity is expressed by the doctrine of intentionality the question is: what is intentionality? Is it subjectivity, that is, is it an expanded "cogito," a "cogito" creating the world, a step that Descartes himself did not take? Or is it, as St. Thomas thinks, a trans-subjective identity with the world? So we have a conflict of problems and a radical debate, it seems to me, between subjectivity and trans-subjectivity as the starting point of philosophizing. I who set out to philosophize, do I philosophize in the manner of Descartes as an isolated self—a thought, i.e. ideas? In that case I shall never reach the world. That is the lesson of Cartesian idealism as taught by Descartes' disciples.

Is the basic phenomenon, as I start out to philosophize, my identity with the world? Is it true that I am in the world in an extraordinary way by a knowing identity? In that situation what do I mean by the "I" when I say: "I know the world"? That "I" is not a Cartesian "I"; it is not isolated thought. That "I" is really an "I" that "includes" the world within it. It is an "I" that returns to itself via the world. But things are not so easy between St. Thomas and Husserl, for Husserl, believing that in some sense knowledge is trans-subjective, as the formula *ego cogito cogitata* clearly suggests, nevertheless wanted to enclose this trans-subjective fact within a Cartesian subjectivity. How could he return to an apodictic starting point for philosophy, to an "I," which grasps itself in the very act of doubting? How could he return to that unless precisely he returned to it as a pure "I," bare of everything. What then happens to trans-subjectivity?

It seems to me that Husserl tried to get a result out of Cartesianism that he could not. You cannot begin with the idea that human consciousness is in a state of identity with the world and then treat that consciousness as though it were a pure and simple subject, a Cartesian "I"; this you cannot do. Nor can you use the doctrine of intentionality as the tool by which that consciousness *makes* the world as part of the expansion of the self. Intentionality is centered in the world, Cartesian consciousness in the self. These two points of view cannot be included in one and the same doctrine. No, it is not possible, and I say that Husserl did not do it unless you want to say that he did it precisely because he made intentionality to be part of an idealistic epistemology. In that case, he really did not identify the self with the world, nor recognize that there was a world there, the other that we know. The only world that exists in the transcendental idealism of Husserl is the one that the transcendental consciousness *makes*. It comes from the inside out; it is not the other. And in that sense, the whole machinery of consciousness, taken from Brentano, has lost its point. It may be true that if you are going to have a twentieth-century Cartesianism you will have to get into the business of eating your cake and having it too.

It seems to me that Husserl has no world after he has reduced it; he has no world because what began as a world, the other, the transcendent, now is merely the creature of the consciousness. That elaborate discussion of inner and outer experience, of immanent and transcendent experience, that elaborate analysis of perception, its piecemeal or perspectival character, that was really intended in principle to do justice to the otherness of the world, given somehow beyond the consciousness, which was not the consciousness but was there mysteriously for the consciousness to come to terms with.

If that whole doctrine of transcendent perception is not intended to come to terms with the given otherness of the world, I really don't know what it is about. And what I am saying is that Husserl's answer not only is not a very good answer to the data of the problem, but it tampers with the data. It tampers with the data in the sense that the transcendence of the world begins by being admitted, and then becomes synthesized by the transcendental consciousness as part of its life. I am wondering, therefore, how you can really maintain the transcendence of the world, and have all the problems with the transcendence of the world that Husserl has, and quite legitimately. Inadequate evidence and so on. How you can do that, if, in the end, this transcendent and hardly encompassable fact is the problem of inner consciousness? Why do you have so much trouble constituting the world when it is after all part of your own life and your consciousness?

I think—I don't want to be difficult or hypercritical—but it seems to me that Husserl on the way to becoming a transcendental idealist denatured the phenomenological data that he began with. The world doesn't remain there in its transcendence, it is altered and the difference between transcendent and immanent perception is precisely that immanent perception is inner and therefore given whole, and outer perception is outer and therefore given piecemeal. Wherein is the world transcendent if it is included within the self-constitution of the consciousness?

So it seems to me that the moment Husserl used the data of intentionality as part of a Cartesian subjectivity synthesizing the world, the moment that happened, all that Husserl had said in the name of transcendence, all that he had done, beginning with bracketing, the neutralizing of the existential claim of the world, all this is gone. It is gone not just in the answer, but also as a problem. He did not really have, from the beginning, a problem that you could call the transcendence of the world. If he had retained the notion of intentionality, if he had centered knowledge in the other, in the world, so as to recognize that intentionality designates the otherness of the knowing act, that it designates the identity of the knower with the known, and that knowing is world-centered, I do not know if Husserl's transcendental idealism would have been possible. But it is only by systematically translating into sub-jective terms all the trans-subjective data that he amassed in examining transcendence, that he succeeds. He succeeds, but, it seems to me, at the price of changing the meaning of his problem, changing from a world-centered doctrine of inten-tionality to a subjectively-centered doctrine, from a doctrine in which to account for the otherness of the world could very well be a problem, to a doctrine in which intentionality, far from carrying the otherness of the world, creates it. *What world is that?*

Perhaps the most serious problem that I see, a problem beyond Husserl, and beyond St. Thomas, too, is whether this return to subjectivity which is the hallmark of Cartesianism and of the modern philosophy that was to follow, is really possible. If I am to believe St. Thomas Aquinas, it seems to me that the basic condition of human consciousness is trans-subjectivity, not subjectivity, its basic condition is its rela-tional identity with the world, its presence in the world. And that which we call subjectivity is a reflexive return to the self after, and on the basis of, trans-subjectivity. I, who in knowing am identical with the world can, within that identity, reflex-ively return to myself and recognize that I am myself, and that the world is the world. But it is within my identity with the world, within trans-subjectivity, that I return to myself.

If one is to go all the way in this problem, one must do what Heidegger did; contest the idea that philosophy begins in subjectivity, i.e. what the last 300 years of philosophy have believed. From Descartes, to the Cartesians, to Kant, to Hegel, the philosophizing "I" is a pure *subject*. Well, Heidegger says it is not; the philosophizing subject is the person who is himself in thought and has this extraordinary meeting with being. The philosophizing subject is at a meeting. He is not a subject. And just as he turned his back on modern subjectivity so he turned his back on modern idealism. Heidegger is no idealist. He may not be a realist, but he is no idealist. So, really, what Husserl poses for us as a problem on the question of intentionality is whether philosophy as a corrected Cartesianism is possible. The original Cartesianism may not be possible, but is a corrected Cartesianism, which begins with a trans-subjective fact, namely my presence in the world, and then sacrifices that fact to subjectivity—is that possible? Well, since people do it, I suppose it is possible. Philosophically, to coin a word, I think it is nonsense.

Center for Thomistic Studies
University of St. Thomas

Ideology and Aquinas

Joseph Owens, C.Ss.R.

I

To confront St. Thomas Aquinas with the notion of ideology is none too easy an undertaking. A chronological wall some five centuries high separates him from ideological vocabulary and framework. Still more significantly, a philosophical wall with foundations reaching down to the very bedrock of human thought stands guard against empathic interpenetration of the two prima facie opposed ways of thinking. They present themselves as radically distinct fashions of understanding the universe and man's function in it. Nevertheless in today's situation, with a widely prevalent tendency to view human aspirations and activity as a struggle between rival ideologies, a look at the difference between ideological thinking and a well-established non-ideological outlook seems quite in order.

First, one may ask, just what does ideology mean? In the course of its comparatively short history the term has been used in a number of different senses. Apart from its dominant significance in regard to ideas as means or tools or weapons for social and political action, it has been taken to mean philosophy in general, or metaphysics, or epistemology, or even a part of logic.[1] It first appears in the literature in 1798, coined by a French nobleman against the turbulent background of the great Revolution. He was Antoine-Louis-Claude Destutt de Tracy. The accumulation of names marks him as belonging to the nobility. The appellation "Tracy" witnesses to remote

Scottish ancestry, though the family had moved permanently from Scotland to France in the fifteenth century. Destutt himself lived from 1754 to 1836. But early in the decade in which he coined the term "ideology" his prospects of so lengthy a lifespan were none too bright. He was imprisoned as a nobleman during the Reign of Terror, and sentenced to the guillotine. He was waiting in prison for his farewell ride on the tumbrel through the streets of Paris when, a few days before the date set for the execution, Robespierre's own head fell at the drop of the revolutionary blade. The Terror was ended, and Destutt lived on to coin the word "ideology" some five years later.

It was in that highly poignant and dramatic setting, then, that the term "ideology" made its appearance. Destutt, having lived through the violent breakdown of the old order, was deeply involved in the reorganization of French education and public life under the Directory. The method to be used was framed in the secularistic mentality of the eighteenth century French intellectuals. It aimed to shape morality and social order not on haphazard experience or religious traditions, but on carefully thought out human ideas. In that project the *study* of ideas was presented as absolutely basic, and was given the new designation "ideology" in the etymological sense of the account (*logos*) or science of ideas.[2]

Taken just in itself the notion of ideology, as the study of ideas, may seem harmless enough, or even attractive. But for its originator it carried with it a readily recognizable conception of what human ideas were considered to be. Destutt took the notion of an idea from Condillac, whom he regarded as having more than anyone else cultivated the soil for ideology and really created the undertaking. Along with Condillac, Destutt looked upon ideas as direct and self-contained objects of the human mind, to be explained not in traditional metaphysical fashion but rather through their psychological and anthropological origins. The mind's ideas were to be observed and analyzed and systematized like the properties of a mineral or plant or animal. Ideology was in consequence classed by Destutt as a part of zoology.[3]

Condillac, in turn, had claimed to be developing the method already used by Locke for dealing with ideas.[4] For Locke, the human mind had no other immediate object than its ideas, "and our (sic) Knowledge is only conversant about them."[5] In accord with this conception of them, Destutt was able to look upon ideas and their liaison as effects of organic movements.[6] Back of Locke, however, was the epistemological revolution effected by Descartes. Before Descartes' time, Western philosophy had regarded human thought as bearing directly and immediately on things other than itself, things outside itself. To break with that ingrained attitude, Descartes inaugurated the severely ascetic discipline of systematic doubt to rid the mind of its trust in sense cognition. Quite as the technique of prolonged meditation in the Jesuit discipline at Laflèche had been meant to turn the mind away from sensible things and focus on spiritual reality, so the Cartesian philosophical meditation was used to center the mind's attention on itself and its ideas instead of on the sensible world. The direct and immediate object of human cognition was in this uncompromising way located in the mind itself and its ideas.[7]

Against that philosophical background the notion of ideology could hardly help but exercise a strong hold on intellectuals bent on reshaping the social and political order. What could be more appealing than a new dawn for the world, emerging not from ignorance and superstition and outworn realities of the past, but from the enlightenment of the ideas worked out in man's finally attained age of reason? The prospect was enticing. Yet Napoleon soon came to regard the thinking of the ideologists as out of touch with reality, while on the philosophical level a traditionalist named Louis Gabriel Ambroise Vicomte de Bonald, born the same year as Destutt (1754), trenchantly criticized the whole ideological undertaking as self-defeating in its approach to human thought. Even though the Cartesian outlook had long since become established in Western philosophical circles, Bonald vigorously reasserted the older conception of the mind as the instrument rather than the object of human cognition. In a vivid metaphor he emphasized the incongruity of mind serving as object. It made the hammer an object to be pounded upon, instead of a tool for pounding on something else.[8]

Epistemologically this consideration remains crucial in a confrontation of ideology with the thought of Aquinas. From the philosophical viewpoint the basic question centers on whether the human mind in some way provides the content of its ideas, or whether it itself and its concepts have rather the role of instruments for directly knowing things external to itself. The fundamental issue in the confrontation is whether reality or human ideas will come first. From the manner in which that underlying metaphysical problem is solved will emerge the respective ways in which ideology on the one hand, and traditional "right reason" on the other, are brought to bear upon the organization and direction of human conduct. This is the problem that the present paper wishes to examine.

II

Historically, as has just been noted, the advent of the Cartesian epistemology marks the chronological point that irrevocably separated in advance the future ideological thinking from the metaphysics and the ethics of Aquinas. In the philosophical tradition that goes back to Aristotle the mind in the actuality of cognition becomes and is the thing known.[9] So identified with real sensible things, the cognitive agent is thereby concomitantly aware of himself, his activity, and his concepts. He can then make these the objects of reflexive cognitional acts. But in those new and subsequent reflexive acts the mental objects remain other than the acts by which they are known. Aristotle could accordingly make universal his assertion that for a human cognitive agent perception and intellection are always of something other than themselves.[10]

In this explanation of cognition, then, the human mind has to become identical with real sensible things before it can know itself. The priority is metaphysical, not temporal, for the instant it knows a sensible thing it is concomitantly aware of itself. But real sensible things are what the human mind basically knows, and it knows itself and its concepts only in terms of its awareness of those real things. Hence the real world, in its existent sensible things, has to be kept basic in all subsequent thinking and reasoning. Human ideas are not the natural basis for human intellectual activity. They are but concepts later made the object of reflexive thought, and when they are set up as independent starting points they are detached from their original basis. They are taken as on their own, apart from the really existent world that is required for their control. There need be little wonder that ideologies can run wild.

Nor does the reduction of ideas to sensations in Locke, Condillac and Destutt at all allow ideology to rejoin the Aristotelian epistemology. Origin of all human knowledge in sensations is not enough. Real sensible things, existent in the external world, and not just sensations existent in the human cognitive agent, are what the Aristotelian explanation shows to be the origin of human cognition. Sensible *things*, not sensations of them, are epistemologically basic. The Aristotelian tradition in philosophy ably sustains the immediate and direct grasp of the real world. Nothing less can satisfy it. Any interjection of ideas or sensations as intermediate objects between itself and the really existent thing is impossible for it. Concepts and sensations are instruments for grasping things other than themselves. Human thought, to be true to its own nature, has to be based solidly upon the real world.[11]

Aquinas made the Aristotelian epistemology his own. Besides, he added a new and remarkable fruitful dimension to its interpretation. While for Aristotle the cognitive agent

became and was the sensible things, for Aquinas, in approach
from the opposite end, the sensible things *existed* cognitionally
in the knower.[12] The explanation was in terms of existence.
Aristotle, in contrast to the Empedoclean situation, emphati-
cally rejected the formulation that the stone is in the soul that
knows it. Only the stone's form, in instrumental fashion, is
in the soul.[13] Aquinas, against the Avicennian background
that a thing existed in reality and in cognition, could readily
speak of cognitional existence in contrast to real existence.
Both types were genuine existence, and both were distinguished from the thing they made exist. This background was
common to medieval thinkers in the Aristotelian tradition.
But Aquinas' entitative distinction between a thing and its
existence enabled him to formulate sharply the Aristotelian
epistemology in terms of one and the same thing acquiring
a new kind of existence in the actuality of cognition. He
was able to give a clearer explanation of how the thing remained exactly the same under the different kinds of existence, whether it was attained in individual or in universal
fashion.

The result is that for Aquinas the real external world
comes to exist within the human knower. So present, it is the
mind's direct and immediate object, and serves as the basis for
correct thinking. No idea or sensation of it comes in between.
From the sensible things directly known the mind proceeds to
cognition about itself and its ideas. The firm foundation in
reality is never lost, as long as the mind reasons correctly. In
directing human conduct, therefore, Aquinas' "right reason"
(*recta ratio*) never becomes an ideology.

To ask how this epistemology can be proven would be to
throw the question back into the Cartesian approach. It would
be presuming that you first know objects other than really existent sensible things, objects such as ideas or sensations or
eternal truths, and are asking how you may infer from them
the existence of things corresponding to them outside the
mind. Rather, the real existence of sensible things in themselves, outside the mind, is known in priority to all epistem-

ology, and in priority to all presuppositions that the human mind can make. Really existent sensible things are the natural starting point for all human thinking. They are primitively and unshakably present to the mind. Read the Western philosophers carefully and you will find that not one of them had the least real doubt that he was living in a sensible world other than himself and his ideas, and that he was talking to and writing for real persons other than himself. Locke would never have any controversy with somebody who claimed to doubt Locke's existence, since that person could never be sure that Locke was saying something contrary to his opinion.[14] Hume, when the real world seemed to melt away under his phenomenalistic speculations, would turn away from them for the time being, have a good dinner and enjoyable conversation with his friends, play a game of backgammon, and again find himself ready to live, talk and act like other people in ordinary life.[15] Even the Greek Skeptics, who doubted all dogmatic philosophy, are reported by Diogenes Laertius (IX, 103) as recognizing without hesitation that it was day and that they were alive, as well as many other manifest things in life. You just cannot shake that immediately manifest foundation for all natural human knowledge. It is there as the starting point, and is the starting point not primarily because it is perceived or is known or is true, but first and foremost because it *exists* in itself.

Existent sensible things, not sensations of them, are therefore epistemologically basic and prior for Aquinas. This is far from a naive realism. It is a highly developed metaphysics of cognition. It cannot even be described as a realism, if "realism" is taken to mean reasoning from ideas or sense data to the existence of corresponding or correlative external things. Properly, it is beyond epistemological designation, since all human knowledge, epistemology included, originates in sensible things. It is a question of existence, the existence that things have in cognition.[16] It calls accordingly for designation in a sphere wider than that of epistemology. In regard to the present topic it requires that all human thinking be solidly based upon the real world. It does not tolerate the detaching of concepts from this basis and using them as independent ideas for regulating human conduct.

III

The impenetrable philosophical wall between ideology and Aquinas, then, is obvious enough in the radical contrast between their respective conceptions of the direct object of human thought. From that basic difference proceed the two divergent ways in which human knowledge is related to moral, social and political action. For ideology, human thought is philosophically an absolute beginning, and is accordingly meant for what comes after it. For Aquinas, human thought is subsequent to external reality, and the external world is meant to further it. Fundamentally, the cleavage between the two ways of thinking is fully that sharp.

For ideology, thought in its entirety is meant for action. Although Destutt himself regarded ideas—something mental —as the theme of ideology, he did so expressly with a view towards their use for education and the organization of social and political life. In the mainstream of the ideological thought that flowed through the nineteenth and twentieth centuries, the interest has been in the relation of thought to action, either for organizing and stimulating and promoting social activity, or for disguising the real motivation of some policy, or for using ideas as weapons, for or against, in the ongoing Marxist dialectic. Throughout all the variations in this mainstream, ideology has regularly considered the bearing on practical activity to be essential to it. Thought is meant for action.

With Aquinas, in direct contrast, action in its entirety is meant for intellectual contemplation. Aristotle had long since located the ultimate purpose of human living, both individual and social, in intellectual contemplation of the mind's highest object.[17] What that object is, he did not specify further. Commentators may particularize it for him as the pursuit of intellectual life in the arts and sciences, or as metaphysical contemplation, or as the highest self-knowledge quite in the manner of cognition in the Aristotelian separate substances. The Aristotelian conception was open to all of this. It was open, too, to the beatific vision of God as probed in Christian theology. Human destiny was eternal life, which consisted in knowing God (Jn. 17, 3). In this way the infinite good that alone can satisfy fully the human intellect and the human will was to be possessed. In Aristotle all practical life, called by him (E N, X 8,1178a-9-10) the life of virtue was indeed happiness but only in a secondary degree. It was happiness, in fact, *because* of its nature it was meant to bring about the conditions for intellectual contemplation. For Aquinas, with his further vision set upon eternal life, all contemplative as well as practical activity upon earth formed correspondingly but an imperfect and secondary type of happiness. It was happiness only insofar as it is a way (*via*) to the perfect beatitude found in the vision of God after bodily death.[18] But the overall relation of the practical to the contemplative remained the same. Just as for Aristotle "we do business in order that we may have leisure, and carry on war in order that we may have peace" (E N, X 7,1177b4-6; Rackham trans.), so for Aquinas all political life and activity is undertaken in order to bring about the conditions for "contemplating truth" (*In X Eth.*, lect. 11, Spiazzi no. 2101).

According to this conception, then, we live, toil, struggle, take recreation, organize society and wage war in order that we may be able to *think*. Practical life, for Aquinas as well as for Aristotle, is though in different ways meant for thought. In ideology, in contrast, thought is meant for practical activity. The advance of Aquinas over Aristotle was due to his Christian belief and Christian theology. But in both thinkers, the fundamental orientation of practical activity towards thought persists unabated. In Aquinas the appeal is much stronger, provided his religious beliefs be accepted. The state of supreme contemplation becomes open to all men and women, regardless of intellectual gifts or opportunities during

an earthly lifespan. It is not reserved for the very few who
have high intellectual endowment and are fortunate enough
to enjoy the required conditions as they live on through the
maturity of a full natural life. It is not at all denied on its
primary level to those who spend a lifetime in devoted toil and
hardship or poverty. It shows tellingly how contemplation is
not something thin or wan or of ivory tower character.
Rather, since knower and known are identical in the act of
cognition, it makes the seeing of God in the beatific vision
face to face mean the fully satisfying possession of unlimited
good. It means having everything that one could rationally
desire, since all things, no matter what they are or where they
are, have their highest type of existence in the divine creative
essence.[19] They are all possessed in the closest possible union
that can be had with them, the union of cognition. In a word,
the beatific vision is seen to be in the highest degree the
possession and enjoyment of everything desirable. It is presented as an object worthy to be striven for in all practical life,
and to be regarded as something far greater and more sublime
than the practical activity meant for its attainment. Contemplation is in this way explained convincingly as the supreme
goal of all human activity, individual, social, and political. Instead of thought being meant for practical activity, as in ideology, all practical activity is ultimately meant for thought.

IV

The outlook of Aquinas, then, differs radically from
ideology in the supreme place it assigns to theoretical knowledge. But for Aquinas, again in the wake of Aristotle, there
are two other types of knowledge. One is practical knowledge,
meant to guide conduct. The other is the type of knowledge
found in the arts and crafts, and meant for production.[20] In
both these types, knowledge is meant for activity outside itself. Can either of these types be equated with ideology?

As regards practical knowledge, Aristotle had located its source in human choice, choice that was guided by right reason (*orthos logos*). Reason was "right" when it conformed with proper habituation in the moral agent, habituation acquired by correct education from earliest childhood. A person so brought up in the virtues will make the correct moral judgment in each particular case, as circumstances keep changing. In this way the criterion of moral goodness is not some preconceived idea, but the individual judgments made in each case by the virtuous man. Moral or practical philosophy is built upon these judgments. It garners its premises from them, and from these premises draws conclusions that correspond to them in nature.[21] In a word, it is built not on theoretically conceived ideas, but upon the lived moral experience of individual moral agents.

Again Aquinas makes this Aristotelian conception of moral philosophy his own. The moral order is made by human reason in its consideration of the activities of the will.[22] It is not set up through ideas conceived in independence of actual human decisions. Rather, the "right reason" (*recta ratio*) that determines what should be done is prudence, as it was with Aristotle.[23] It does not function as an idea, but as a judgment made in conformity with correctly habituated rational inclination,[24] in accord with the incessantly changing situation of each moment. "Right reason," so understood, gives rise to moral absolutes, such as the wrongness of adultery, theft or murder, (Aristotle, *E N*, II 7,1107a11-17), and requires stable habituation and enforced laws for public order and education. But it rests ultimately upon the individual moral judgments, and not upon preconceived ideas. In practice the extremely important result is that the needs of a dominant ideology can never override the individual prudent judgment of a morally good person. A citizen is not morally obliged to submit to tyranny, nor a child to betray parents, in the interests of an ongoing dialectic.

The comparative length of the Second Part of the *Summa theologiae*, and the numerical predominance of manuscripts

of the Second Part of that Second Part in the epoch immediately following the death of Aquinas, attest his interest in
making knowledge of the virtues and vices bear directly on
practical life.[25] His conception of practical philosophy as a
type of knowledge meant entirely for conduct is fully as strong
as that of an ideologist. As with Aristotle (*E N*, VII
3,1147a26-31) its philosophical reasonings have their conclusions in action. But likewise with Aristotle (a22; cf. I
3,1095a2-11) their *premises* have to be ingrown through experience and habituation. Ideas, just in themselves, are not
enough to ground moral conduct. Accordingly the connection
of practical philosophy with action is even stronger in Aquinas
than in ideology. His practical philosophy may resemble an
ideology insofar as its source is internal to the moral agent.
Yet it differs radically from an ideology insofar as that source
is located in the individual moral judgments and not in pre-
established ideas or plans.

But will not these considerations allow ideology to be
assimilated to the fourth type of human knowledge listed by
Aquinas in the opening paragraph (ed. Cathala no. 1) of his
work on the *Nicomachean Ethics?* In that type of knowledge
the source is internal to the agent, and is now a fixed design
or plan in accordance with which the activity takes place.
Ideology has in fact been equated with an art understood in
this Aristotelian sense.[26] May not ideology, then, be admitted
into the Thomistic conception of the sciences as the direction
of human conduct after the fashion of an Aristotelian art?

Undoubtedly the resemblance here becomes much closer
than in the cases of either theoretical or practical philosophy.
Yet the equation is far from complete. The traditional notion
of an art requires the working of a design or conception into
something that functions as matter for it, as the design in a
blueprint is worked into the wood or mortar or stone to make
a house, or as the musical or poetic inspiration is worked into
sounds or imaginations. Free choice can hardly be regarded as
matter in this sense. It does not lie before the agent as
something capable of being worked into a form. Rather, it is

to be guided into making the correct moral judgment. As itself the source of moral philosophy, it was radically distinguished by Aristotle (*Metaph.*, E 1, 1025b22-24) from the conceptual or technical origin of productive knowledge. From this viewpoint it is something new in each individual case. It is not repetitive, like the design in art. Some arts, such as medicine and navigation, require a great deal of adaptation in working out their set plan. But in the realm of free choice there is no set plan to be worked out. Ideology may insist on the dynamic flexibility of its patterns. But patterns there are.[27] No such patterns, regardless of how flexible they may be, are able to mold human conduct in the way an artistic design is worked into its appropriate matter. Even the notion of a blueprint for social organization strikes most ideologists as an incongruity, though it is urged against them pejoratively by their opponents. Ideology does not conform to the notion of productive knowledge that is recognized by Aquinas, despite the fact that it resembles that type more closely than in the case of the other two.

The conclusion, in consequence, is that ideology does not fit into any of the three types of philosophy found in the tradition of Aquinas. To make a place for it in the philosophical world, the new starting point of Descartes in mind and ideas is required. There, ideas may be viewed as basic in themselves from the epistemological viewpoint and already constituted for application to human conduct. This conception is inadmissible in the Aristotelian tradition, where sensible things are the origin of all theoretical knowledge and choice the source of all moral premises.

V

But if ideology differs so radically from all three types of knowledge as accepted by Aquinas, how can there be any dialogue between the two ways of thinking? Chronologically, Aquinas lived far too soon to leave any confrontation with ideology in his writings. In this respect the chronological wall is insurmountable. Yet his thought remains in those who read him, and today they come face to face with ideology. There can still be doctrinal confrontation, as the fact of debates between Thomists and Marxists on labor unions, education, marriage, abortion, genocide and so many other questions shows. How is this possible, if the respective ways of thinking are so radically different? Does there still remain any common ground for profitable discussion?

There certainly is a common ground. The intelligible content of the Thomistic concept and of the ideological idea are the same—man, animal, earth, star, galaxy, family, friendship, soviet, nation and so on. Both sides are talking about the same things and drawing conclusions from their intelligible content. For Aquinas this is the common nature or nature taken absolutely, which has real existence in things and intentional existence in cognition.[28] Through the concept it exists cognitionally in the human mind. Reflexively the mind can make this concept the object of a new act of cognition. As object of the reflexive cognition the concept achieves the status of an idea. In the wake of four centuries of Cartesian tradition the mistake is easily made of detaching the idea from its epistemological base and allowing it to function as the immediate object of human thought. Its intelligible content, however, remains exactly the same and furnishes common ground for discussion and controversy.

This common ground will allow many identical conclusions to be reached by both sides, for instance in the natural, life and social sciences. But in metaphysics, for instance on the existence of God, the divergence will be great when the respective starting points are ideas and real things. Likewise in moral and political philosophy the way of conceiving society will differ crucially as one bases practical reasoning on ideas or on the freedom of the individual human person. Here there will be no possibility of doctrinal agreement, but only—may it be hoped—on conventional adjustment. To maintain itself in practice an ideology has to give reality the preference over its own notions, for instance in increasing repressive power rather than letting the state wither away, and in the copious use of rewards and penalties instead of relying on ideological motivation. Dialogue may continue with profit in many spheres. But the overall stands will remain the same, unless the basic habituation of the respective participants undergoes change.[29] The ideologist will continue to regard traditional philosophers as victims of pitiably naive realism. He in turn will appear against the background of Aquinas as radically misunderstanding the origin and nature of ideas, and as attempting the unrewarding task so tellingly expressed in Bonald's metaphor of pounding upon the hammer rather than using it as a tool for profitable construction.

Pontifical Institute of Mediaeval Studies
Toronto

NOTES

1. In a Neoscholastic manual widely used in the last half of the nineteenth century the subdivision of logic that studied the origin of ideas was named *ideologia*—Gaetano Sanseverino, *Elementa philosophiae christianae*, 2nd ed. (Naples: Bibliotheca Catholica, 1873), I, 442. This use of the term did not survive, though its background was the problematic of ideas as found in Descartes and Locke. On the uses of it that did survive, see Karl Mannheim, *Ideology and Utopia*, trans. Louis Wirth and Edward Shils (New York: Harcourt, Brace and Company, 1936), pp. 49-80; Arne Naess, *Democracy, Ideology and Objectivity* (Oslo: University Press, 1956), pp. 141-161; Keith Bruce Miller, *Ideology and Moral Philosophy* (New York: Humanities Press, 1971), pp. 27-36. An extensive bibliography on ideology may be found in Ferruccio Rossi-Landi, *L'ideologia* (Milan: Instituto Editoriale Internazionale, 1978), pp. 246-345.

2. See Antoine-Louis-Claude Destutt Comte de Tracy, *Eléments d'idéologie*, 3rd ed. (Paris, Courcier, 1817; Reprint, Paris: Vrin, 1970), I, p. 12 of Gouhier's "Introduction historique." The new epoch in human thought "doit être appelée l'ère francaise"— Destutt, II, 395.

3. Destutt, *Eléments*, I, xiii. Cf.: ". . . ayant une *existence absolue*, au moins dans notre esprit," II, 397.

4. Etienne Bonnot de Condillac, *An Essay on the Origin of Human Knowledge*, trans. Thomas Nugent (London: J. Nourse, 1756. Reprint, New York: AMS Press, 1974), p. i. Texts supporting these references may be found listed in Joseph Owens, "Is Philosophy in Aristotle an Ideology?" in *Ideology, Philosophy and Politics*, ed. Anthony Parel (Waterloo, Ont.: Wilfrid Laurier University Press, 1983), nn. 2-5.

5. John Locke, *An Essay Concerning Human Understanding*, IV, 1, 1; ed. Peter H. Nidditch (Oxford: Clarendon Press, 1975), p. 525. Even from today's vantage point the ideological function of ideas as objects has not gone unnoticed: "Le mot même—'idéologie'

150

—est né . . . pour désigner une analyse des idées prises comme des objets." Michel Amiot, in *Les idéologies dans le monde actuel*, ed. Jean Onimus (Paris: Desclée de Brouwer, 1971), p. 18.

6. ". . . des mouvemens (sic) organiques qui produisent nos idées." Destutt, I, 262.

7. René Descartes, *Meditations*, II, trans. Haldane and Ross, *The Philosophical Works of Descartes* (Cambridge: University Press, 1911-1912), I, 157.

8. ". . . labeur ingrat, et sans résultat possible, qui n'est autre chose que frapper sur le marteau." Bonald, *Recherches philosophiques*, in *Oeuvres*, 4th ed. (Brussels: Société Nationale, 1845), V, 40—41. The metaphor seems to have been original with Bonald.

9. Aristotle, *De an.*, III,8,431b20-23; cf. 5,430a19-20.

10. *Metaph.*, Lambda 9,1074b35-36. Cf. traditional text at *De an.*, III,4,429b5-10. In the *Metaphysics* passage, Aristotle is regarding the commonly accepted notion of cognition as an aporia he has to face in maintaining the self-knowledge of the separate forms.

11. Further discussion may be found in Joseph Owens, "The Primacy of the External in the Thomistic Noetics," *Eglise et Théologie*, V (1974), 189-205.

12. ". . . cognitio . . . dicit existentiam cogniti in cognoscente." Aquinas, *De ver.*, II, 5, ad 15m; ed. Leonine, XXII, 64.421-424. Cf. *In Lib. de causis*, Prop. 18; ed. Saffrey, p. 101.14-16.

13. Aristotle, *De an.*, III,8,431b28-432a3. Aristotle's point is that the means for bringing about cognition are not the Empedoclean elements but the form of the sensible thing, a form used by the soul as its instrument for knowing the external thing. For further discussion, see my article "Form and Cognition in Aristotle," *Ancient Philosophy*, I, (1980), 17-27.

14. Locke, *Essay*, IV, 11, 3; ed. P. H. Nidditch, p. 631.

15. Hume, *A Treatise of Human Nature*, I, 4, 7; ed. L.A. Selby-Biggs, rev. P. H. Nidditch (Oxford: Clarendon Press, 1978), p. 269.

16. For Aquinas a finite nature just in itself, or as absolutely considered, has no existence at all. It can have existence either in reality or in cognition. See *De ente et essentia*, III; ed. Leonine, XLIII, 374.26-72.

17. Aristotle, *E N*, X,7,1177a12-1178a8. Cf. *Metaph.*, A 2,982a30-b4.

18. "Contemplatio autem Dei est duplex. Una per creaturas,

quae imperfecta est, ratione jam dicta, in qua contemplatione Philosophus . . . felicitatem contemplativam posuit, quae tamen est felicitas viae." Aquinas, *In Sent.*, Prol., q. 1, a. 1, Solut.; ed. P. Mandonnet, I, 7-8.

19. "Unde uniuscuiusque naturae causatae *prima* consideratio est secundum quod est in intellectu divino; *secunda* vero consideratio est ipsius naturae absolute; *tertia* secundum quod habet esse in rebus ipsis, vel in mente angelica; *quarta* secundum esse quod habet in intellectu nostro." *Quodl.*, VIII, 1, 1; ed. R. Spiazzi.

20. Aquinas, *In I Eth.*, lect. 1, Spiazzi nos. 1-2.

21. Aristotle, *E N*, I,3,1094b14-22. Cf. II,2,1104a1-10.

22. ". . . ordo quem ratio considerando facit in operationibus voluntatis." Aquinas, *In I Eth.*, lect. 1; ed. Leonine, XLVII, 4.20-22.

23. Aristotle, *E N*, VI,13,1144b27-28. Cf. Aquinas "Cum enim prudentia sit recta ratio agibilium," *ST*, I-II, 56, 3; ". . . prudentia vero est recta ratio agibilium," 57, 4; and 58, 4.

24. Aristotle, *E N*, III,4,1113a29-33; VI,2,1139a23-31; b12-13. On the role of affective judgment in Aquinas, cf. Rafael-Thomas Caldera, *Le jugement par inclination chez Saint Thomas d'Aquin* (Paris: Vrin, 1980), pp. 131-135.

25. On this question see the Gilson Lecture of Leonard Boyle, *The Setting of the Summa theologiae of Saint Thomas*, Etienne Gilson Series 5 (Toronto: Pontifical Institute of Mediaeval Studies, 1982).

26. "Metaphysics would cease to be systematic, theoretical, or science. It would become an art; it would be ideology." Oliver Martin, *Metaphysics and Ideology* (Milwaukee: Marquette University Press, 1959), p. 33.

27. See Naess, pp. 226-233; cf. p. 2.

28. See supra, n. 16. As common, the nature itself remains the same under both types of existence.

29. Aristotle's insistence on the basic role of habituation for moral philosophy is well-known. The dependence of theoretical philosophy on the habituation handed down by others is noted by him at *Metaph.*, a 1,993b14 and 3,994b32-995a3.

Index